FROM A GIN PALACE
TO A KING'S PALACE

Provincial Music Hall in Preston

IT'S A BIT OF A RUIN THAT CROMWELL KNOCKED ABOUT A BIT.

Words by
Harry Bedford
and Terry Sullivan.

Music by
HARRY BEDFORD

Sung by

MISS MARIE LLOYD.

FROM A GIN PALACE TO A KING'S PALACE

Provincial Music Hall in Preston

DAVID JOHN HINDLE

with contributions from Betty Driver, MBE and Sir Tom Finney, OBE, CBE

TEMPUS

This work is dedicated to the memory of my late parents, Joan and Norman Hindle, who took me along to music-hall and pantomime performances at the Royal Hippodrome and King's Palace theatres and to most of Preston's cinemas.

Frontispiece: Considered by many to be the greatest music-hall icon of all time: Miss Marie Lloyd, who appeared at the Preston Hippodrome in November 1911. (Courtesy of P.Vickers)

First published 2007

Tempus Publishing
Cirencester Road, Chalford,
Stroud, Gloucestershire, GL6 8PE
www.tempus-publishing.com

Tempus Publishing is an imprint of NPI Media Group

British Library Cataloguing in Publication Data.
A catalogue record for this book is available from the British Library.

ISBN 978 0 7524 4453 6

Typesetting and origination by NPI Media Group
Printed in Great Britain

The Programme

Acknowledgements

The author and publishers have made every effort to identify and contact copyright holders, and apologise if any acknowledgement has been omitted. It has been a privilege to share experiences with a host of helpful and interesting people, including eminent historians and veterans of the music-hall stage. Accordingly I extend my sincere thanks to those who have recalled popular entertainment in Preston. The former music-hall and iconic television star Betty Driver, MBE, has kindly written the foreword, and football legend Sir Tom Finney has willingly made a contribution with his personal recollections of Preston's music halls.

A big thank you to leading historians Professors Dave Russell and John Walton, Department of Humanities, University of Central Lancashire for their staying power; the late Major A. Burt-Briggs of Lytham, who has provided invaluable information of the syndicate contribution to music hall managed by his ancestors W.H. Broadhead & Sons; Stephen Halliwell, Peter Vickers and members of Preston Historical Society for their support; Christine Dodding for her excellent artistry; Ann Dennison and staff, Harris Reference Library, Preston; Laura Briggs, Harris Museum and Art Gallery, Preston; the *Lancashire Evening Post* for the use of photographs. I am very grateful to the County Archivist at Lancashire Record Office and his staff who kindly gave permission to reproduce important primary sources of material. The Beattie paintings, photographed by Andrew Mather especially for this book, are reproduced by courtesy of the Jesuit Community at St Wilfrid's, Preston.

May we introduce your music-hall chairman, David Hindle. Following *Twice Nightly: An Illustrated History of Entertainment in Preston* (1999), he now presents a complete change of programme chronicling the history of Preston's music halls – just enjoy the type of family show to which a courageous gentleman may safely take his wife. Raise the safety curtain: Maestro, take the cue!

Foreword by Betty Driver, MBE

I am pleased to write this foreword for David Hindle's well-researched book on 'The Good Old Days of Music Hall'. Mr Hindle has compiled a detailed history of the northern music-hall era covering two centuries and this book will undoubtably appeal to all those interested in Preston and its entertainment heritage including historians and students studying the evolution of theatre and music hall and its association with the social history of the former cotton town.

I played Preston when I was about twelve years of age in revue. It was great, the audience wonderful, but what a terrible shame that the wonderful old music halls are now just a memory. I worked over many years, since I was eleven, in theatres throughout the country in variety, revue, West-End shows, films, radio and of course television. The saddest thing of all is that television finished off music hall forever and they call that progress!

30 May 2007

Left: Betty Driver MBE, a veteran of the music-hall stage.

Below, left and right: Programmes of Betty in variety at Sheffield Empire, 1957.

PROGRAMME PRICE 3d.

PROGRAMME

Week commencing MONDAY, JULY 22nd, 1957

1 OVERTURE — The Empire Orchestra

2 FLACK & MILLS ... ... Dance Team

3 LESTER SHARPE & IRIS — Sharpes the Word

4 THE LADRINGLOS — Looping the Loop

5 BOBBY THOMPSON — North Country Comedian

6 BETTY DRIVER
Radio & Television's Personality Girl
At the Piano: Albert Sadler

INTERMISSION
THE EMPIRE ORCHESTRA
under the direction of MAURICE NEWTON

FULLY LICENSED BARS IN ALL PARTS OF THE THEATRE

PROGRAMME CONTINUED OVERLEAF

Co., Ltd., 24 Old Burlington Street, London, W.1   Phone: GROsvenor 7481 (5 lines)

Preface by your very own Sir Tom Finney, OBE, CBE

The name Tom Finney is known throughout the world as one of the greatest footballers of all time. As a boy I had the privilege of witnessing Sir Tom score some classic goals at Deepdale and still cherish the memory of queuing for his autograph outside Preston North End. After twenty-one years of football, Tom scored 187 goals in the league and twenty-three in the cup and was capped for England seventy-six times, incredibly scoring a record number of thirty goals.

As a proud Prestonian I am interested in all aspects of the town's history. David Hindle's latest book covering the popular entertainment industry fills a niche for many aspects of the history of music hall and gives a real insight into what life was like for an earlier generation. This book contains plenty of original material and is a fascinating read, evoking nostalgic memories as well as being a valuable source of reference to theatre lovers, scholars and historians.

David tells the story of music hall by taking the reader on a journey to the past. For me this journey rekindles childhood memories of growing up in Preston. At the age of five my father took me to watch a Preston North End match. I learned to play football with my friends on a bit of spare land behind our house on the Holme Slack Estate. I remember being taken along to the pantomimes at the old Hippodrome and Palace theatres and, like the scene transformation changes, our flexible pitch could be Treasure Island if we were playing at pirates, Texas if we were playing at cowboys. More often it was Deepdale, the home of Preston North End, or perhaps even the hallowed turf of Wembley? The rest, as they say, is history.

Long before I was born the Victorians created the music hall. Indeed, at Preston's Clarence pub tavern music hall in Grimshaw Street they hailed football with the very first chorus song about Preston North End. The references to players' names have meant that this programme can be dated to 1883-84 as Belger, also known as the 'goalkeeper smasher', never played football again after 1885.

As a family in post-war Preston, we saw a range of music-hall artists on stage, including the hilarious antics of Frank Randle whose trademark was 'I've supped some ale toneeet', and Sandy Powell, well known for his slogan, 'Can you hear me mother?' Fortunately humour prevailed throughout my career and there was no shortage of comedians in the dressing rooms.

When I finished playing professional football in 1960 my wage was £20 a week in the season, plus bonuses of £2 for a win and £1 for a draw. For international games I was paid £50. In the summer, the closed season, I drew £17 a week. At the time, there was a story doing the rounds, the truth of which cannot be verified, that Tommy Docherty, one of my teammates, went to the management and complained that he was receiving less money than I was. 'But Tom Finney's a better player than you are,' they told him. 'Not in the close season', retorted the Doc, who was rarely stuck for an answer even then – happy days.

Clarence Music Hall,

GRIMSHAW STREET, PRESTON.

Proprietor - - - - - HARRY HARKER.

OPEN EVERY EVENING AT 7-0, SATURDAY AT 6 O'CLOCK.

THE PLACE TO SPEND A CONVIVIAL HOUR.

Great Success of the

PRESTON HAND-BELL RINGERS,

Six in number, will play some choice selections with their beautiful Peal of 104 Silver Toned Bells.
A treat to all lovers of Music.

Terrific success of the

BROTHERS MILTON,

The best Song and Dance Artistes in Lancashire.   Come and see them.

MR. FRED EDWARDS,

THE COMIC VOCALIST.

Also your Old Friend and Favourite

MR. G. B. BROWNE,

The Author and Composer of the following great Football Song, as sung nightly by him with great success.

Song—"The North End Football Team."

The noble game of football is all the rage you'll own,
And lately in that kind of sport, Proud Preston she has shown ;
That in her town, she does posses, the men I'm proud to say
Who now can play and beat some of the crack teams of the day

CHORUS
Then hurrah for the North End Football team,
To try and win the English cup they mean,
We will dance and sing with joy when they win the final tie ;
Shout hurrah for the North End Football team.

We've Dewhurst on the Left Wing, and Smalley by his side,
With the Ball between them, down the field they very quickly
     glide.
There's Belger in the centre, the favourite of all,
The lad that put's the shakers on the keepers of the goal.
CHORUS : Shout Hurrah, &c.

With Drummond on the Right Wing and the famous Gordon to,
In the whole United Kingdom their equals are but few,
With Russell, Wilson, Robinson, I'm sure it is a treat ;
When Russell's on the Leather, with his Indiarubber feet.
CHORUS.—Shout Hurrah, &c.

There's Duckworth at the back, his play is good none can deny,
And many is the time that he's protected Billy Joy ;
Led on by Ross the Captain. and all admit and say,
That Ross is now the finest back in England to day.
CHORUS.—Shout Hurrah, &c.

So let us wish them all success and coupled with it too,
Their umpire Mr Sudell, their friend so staunch and true,
Long life and luck attend their lot wherever they may be ;
And may the team take good advice from one that is Jim Lee.
CHORUS.—Shout Hurrah, &c.

This Song is copyright, and the sole property of Mr. G. B. Browne.

Proprietor - HARRY HARKER. | Chairman - Mr. G. B. BROWNE. | Pianist - Mr. J. PORTER

ADMISSION FREE.

Children in arms not admitted unless brought by someone.   Seats not guaranteed after 11 p.m.

Choice Wines, Spirits, Ales, Old Ben, &c.   Football Cigars of the Finest Brand.

Barrett and Parkinson, Printers and Stationers, 31, Church Street, Preston.

Clarence music-hall programme, c. 1883–84.

And now for your complete edification, a historiography of music hall

Popular entertainment and the genre of music hall is an important aspect of social history but with certain exceptions the coverage of Edwardian music hall outside London is relatively understudied. A principal aim of this book is to see how Preston fits into the mainstream development of music hall during the crucial Victorian and Edwardian periods, thereby placing Preston within the historiography of the music-hall genre. Accounts of music hall were originally the province of literary and theatre historians and many of the early histories of music hall are little more than personal anecdotal accounts contained in journals. It was not until the latter part of the twentieth century that social and academic historians began to take close interest in music hall.

The Oxford English Dictionary defines music hall as a 'hall used for musical performances; a hall licensed for singing, dancing and other entertainments exclusive of dramatic performances. Russell's definition of music hall covers three key aspects in consideration of the term music hall, and he defines the term 'music hall' as being used in at least three separate ways: 'To describe a certain performance style, an entire section of the entertainment industry or an individual building... It was essentially from the singing saloons that music hall emerged... For this reason no accurate count of halls can be made,' a problem which is applicable to Preston. 'Singing saloons and prototype music halls also went under the names concert room, concert hall and by the 1860s the term music hall appears to have won the day.' He considers that the growth of music hall is 'one of the most striking features of nineteenth-century history'.[1]

Kift explores the conflict between music hall and such controlling forces as local and central government as well as the competition with legitimate theatre.[2] Kift notes that up to her study the 'focus of interest has been almost exclusively on the London halls.' Her work is also based on case studies of Bolton, Leeds, Glasgow, Liverpool, Sheffield and Manchester. Vicinus sees music hall progressing from a class-based to a mass entertainment, a development that can be seen in terms of a complete professional performance and the provision of entertainment for the masses rather than an expression of working-class culture itself.[3] Stedman-Jones[4] regards music hall as being largely confined to the working class while Russell's view is that, 'in class terms, the backbone of the audience was probably always the upper working class and the lower middle class.'[5]

Preston's music hall came under pressure not only because of its working-class origins, but also because of its close links with the drinks trade, both of which were factors in its presumed lack of respectability, if not outright immorality. In relation to this issue, Bailey in *Leisure and Class in Victorian England* examines the transformation of popular leisure from 1830 to 1885 and middle-class schemes for respectability and rational recreation, which attempted to reform the leisure habits of the working classes.[6] Bratton debates the culture of music hall itself by focusing upon class, gender and the songs and sketches that made up the music-hall repertoire.[7]

This work will examine how both reform and performance styles broadened the appeal of music hall until it became a mass entertainment in the Edwardian era.

In the introduction to *Music Hall: The Business of Pleasure*, Bailey reviews several different approaches to music-hall's history. He considers 'music hall's equivalent of the Whig or Liberal interpretation of history', in which proprietors are depicted as benevolent providers of respectable entertainment and the 'idealist interpretation' in which, retrospectively, music hall is seen as either part of the world of the 'Good Old Days' or as a romanticised expression of authentic working-class culture. Bailey shows how social historians have become interested in the halls, viewing them as part of working-class culture but within a capitalist society, so that its development from pothouse to palace is represented as 'a product of conflict rather than consensus.' Earl's national study of the architectural development of music hall describes seven evolutionary phases from the earliest form to the Edwardian variety theatre.[8]

One particularly important local study is Poole's work on Bolton, which examines music hall as part of a growing leisure industry. As well as discussing the influence of respectability, he considers how, as music hall developed and as economic circumstances improved, it began to attract a wider audience, including 'relatively well off shopkeepers and assistants, skilled workers and clerks'. He finds music hall to have been in conflict with local magistrates and in competition with legitimate theatre. An additional significant aspect of his work is the link he explores between circus and music hall.[9]

Preston had music hall and legitimate theatre in direct competition for audiences. In this respect, Reid's findings on the legitimate theatre in Birmingham are helpful in relation to audiences and competition between legitimate theatre and music hall. The legitimate theatre offering Shakespeare and melodrama as well as music hall was popular with the working classes in both towns and the pit and gallery segregated audiences[10], although it would be probably be an over-confident assumption to conclude that higher priced tickets always attracted the upper classes.

Crump's study is a local case history of music hall in Leicester, in which he looks at the social and economic factors influencing development and makes comparisons with the national pattern of growth.[11] His examination of the impact of the national trend of rational recreation on popular culture in Leicester provides an example for the assessment of the influence of the same trend in Preston as part of a consideration of patterns and types of opposition to music hall.

A further local study is Waters' history of the Palace of Varieties in Manchester in which he looks at the complex area of music-hall licensing and the effective strength of antagonism from reformists to the licensing of the Manchester Palace.[12] Conflict resulting from the efforts of social reformers to deflect audiences away from music hall through the promotion of temperance and respectability is presented to strengthen the argument of how music hall was shaped in Preston.

Russell on the Edwardian era advocates the view that the variety theatre was not a lesser form of true music hall, but 'a significant entertainment form in its own right,' with a distinctive 'cultural role and meaning'.[13] His view of the distinctive nature of Edwardian theatre is adopted here as part of the consideration of music hall in Preston in its later form.

The extensive coverage of both Victorian and Edwardian music hall to some extent differentiates this book from similar studies. Mellor's account of the history of regional music hall is one of the few twentieth-century studies with a particular focus on performers, halls and syndication.[14]

Research has utilised a wide range of both secondary and primary sources. *The Preston Chronicle* (1812), *Preston Pilot* (1825), *Preston Guardian* (1844 – founded by temperance advocate, Joseph Livesey) and the *Lancashire Daily Post* have all been scrutinised for material. Reports in the

Right: Julie Andrews in revue at Blackpool Hippodrome, 1949.

Below: Before she hit the big time: Julie Andrews features with her 'Melody of Youth', along with Jimmy Jewel, Ben Warris and Josef Locke.

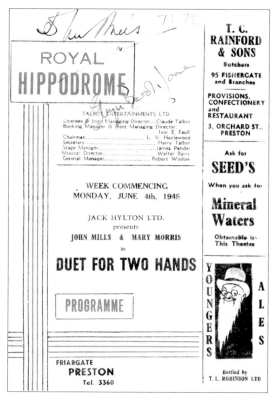

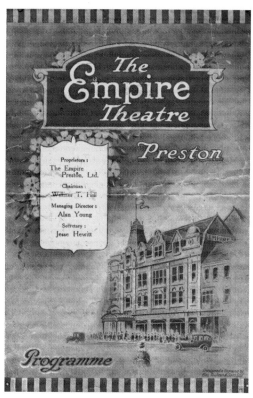

Above left: John Mills signed this Preston Royal Hippodrome programme whilst touring the provinces in 1941.

Above right: This 1920s Preston Empire theatre programme was marked with the inscription 'Your supper's in the oven', probably written by an inconsolable spouse!

Whig paper *The Preston Chronicle* and the *Preston Guardian* were usually prejudiced against music hall because of its association with the drinks trade, whilst the Tory *Preston Pilot* newspaper, with a vested interest in the trade, was generally supportive. National periodicals devoted to the halls and utilised here include *The Era*, published between 1838 and 1939, *The Stage*, first published in 1881, and *The Performer*, first published in 1906.

As a primary source, theatre programmes speak volumes, embracing contemporary comment and evidence of the socio-economic conditions of the time in addition to admission prices, the topography of the theatre, advertisements reflecting the local trading, and of course, the top of the bill and aspiring performers.

The Overture: Maestro, Take the Cue!

The story of music hall in Preston begins inside a singing saloon of a busy smoke-filled public house during the early Victorian era. Centre stage right is a piano with a group of men singing and a woman clog dancing. Outside there are a number of urchins playing in the street between rows of terraced houses and a grey backcloth with a large iron mill gate leading to a yard with numerous chimneys dominating the Preston skyline.

Throughout England, performance styles developed in gin palaces, beer shops and singing saloons in pub taverns around the mid-nineteenth century and culminated in the building of concert halls or music halls. Generic music hall reached its pinnacle during the late Victorian and Edwardian eras in the new lavish, purpose-built variety theatres. After the First World War a downward spiral is apparent culminating in the industry being finally confined to the annals of social history during the mid-twentieth century. Although Preston had its own characteristics, it broadly follows the national pattern of growth with the opening of the Gaiety Palace Theatre of Varieties in 1882 and finally the syndicate-owned King's Palace Theatre in 1913. Consequently, the level of progression may be seen to equate with the notion, 'from a gin palace to a King's Palace,' or, metaphorically speaking, from ugly duckling to beautiful swan.

The main outcome of the closure of the Victorian music halls in Preston led to the syndicates taking an interest in the town. The entertainment industry of the twentieth century was dominated by the success of the music halls. The Manchester-based firm of W.H. Broadhead & Son opened the Royal Hippodrome in 1905 and the King's Palace in 1913. 'The Battle for the King's Palace,' coincided with a surplus of seats for music hall when rival theatre owners raised objections to the licensing application of William Henry & Son for a brand new theatre. But this was part of the Broadhead syndicate's management philosophy in expanding their music halls with Palaces, Empires and Hippodromes to cater for the demand for this genre of popular culture and consequently the battle was won.

I was lucky to be born during the heyday of Preston's cinemas and at a time when the two major theatres, the Royal Hippodrome and the King's Palace, were enjoying a short-lived boom before the onset of the final curtain during the 1950s while the old Empire Music Hall had long switched from safety curtain to silver screen. Regular attendance at most of these venues has helped to stimulate my interest. Even now, half a century later, an enduring memory of the King's Palace is when I stood on the stage of the permanently 'dark' theatre at the eleventh hour and marvelled at the architectural Edwardian splendour surrounding the cavernous auditorium with two large gaping boxes either side of the majestic proscenium. No seats of rich crimson plush, only debris, but where carpets of rose-de-barri pink once provided a tasteful floor covering I collected some old programmes strewn amongst the debris which epitomised the famous, and not-so-famous die-hard music-hall artists who strove to delight our forebears. The half-light preserved an almost mythical aura in the prevailing silence, giving an atmospheric feel to the deserted theatre.

The pristine auditorium of the King's Palace, Preston at the time of its 1913 opening. (courtesy of Harris Museum and Art Gallery, Preston and Major A. Burt Briggs)

Voice from the Gods

But let us suspend reality, for the ghosts of yesteryear are about to take their cue at Preston's King's Palace variety theatre while awaiting the demolition team during 1959. A voice from the gallery gods, whose identity remains an enigma, suddenly disturbs the dark, dank, eerie silence of the embattled warrior, the King's Palace. Bright lights now transform years of neglect for Preston's music hall into a pristine auditorium which again resounds with the applause of thousands of Prestonians dressed in their Victorian refinery – mothers, fathers, sweethearts, children with smiling faces, servicemen in uniform and the inevitable police constable seated at his desk to ensure good order. In the pit, the maestro's moustache develops a sudden twitch as the orchestral sounds reverberate throughout the house, while the venerable chairman mounts his podium and awaits your devout attention, gavel in hand, before introducing the acts in the finest traditions of music-hall nomenclature:

> Raise the tabs [curtains] for I proudly present the most popular, most scintillating and devastatingly dependable traditional music hall. A cornucopia of captivating conviviality, packed with song and dance, novelty acts, special guest turns, sidesplitting banter, and audience participation for your sincere unmitigated enjoyment and delight to be presented in the wonderful old theatres of Preston. Join in the good clean fun and family entertainment. At the end of the show even Queen Victoria would be amused, I think!

Act one – The Victorian Music Hall

Prologue: 'The Good Old Days of Victorian Music Hall?'

Music hall is often referred to in affectionate terms as the 'good old days'; a term made familiar to many by television broadcasts from the famous Leeds City Varieties Music Hall. During the Victorian and Edwardian eras, generic music hall fulfilled a particular social need for the first train and tram passengers at the height of Preston's nineteenth-century Industrial Revolution. The prevailing social considerations serve as a backcloth to the evolution and development of music hall, and this prologue will test the cliché of 'the good old days' during times of economic hardship and social unrest to see if it had any relevance in Victorian Preston.

At the beginning of the nineteenth century the social, economic and industrial foundation of Preston underwent considerable upheaval, contrasting greatly with the town of the previous century. A visit by Daniel Defoe to Preston in 1724 expresses this transformation: 'Preston is a fine town, and tolerably full of people, but not like Liverpool or Manchester; besides, we come now beyond the trading part of the county. Here is no manufacture; the town is full of attorneys, proctors and notaries.' The town also had its fair share of good looking ladies – Hewitson quotes historian Ray when describing the town in 1758: 'Preston is one of the prettiest retirements in England, the resort of beautiful and agreeable ladies and a large number of gentry, which was unexcelled for the politeness of its inhabitants, and vulgarly called Proud Preston on account of its being a place of the best fashion.' The aristocratic upper and middle classes resided in the town's principal streets: Fishergate, Friargate and Church Street. At the beginning of the Industrial Revolution these residences were taken over by small shopkeepers and the attorneys, bankers and gentlemen of the town moved out to Avenham, fashionable Winckley Square and Fishergate Hill areas, close to the working-class communities situated south of the town centre.

By the time of the Industrial Revolution the textile domestic home industry had been completely transformed by technological advances in yarn spinning by Preston-born Sir Richard Arkwright and his patented water frame. Messrs Collinson and Watson opened the town's first cotton-spinning mill on Moor Lane in 1777, which acted as a catalyst for the mechanisation of the industry, eventually superseding the domestic home industry. The town was at the forefront of automation when John Horrocks opened his first factory in 1790, closely followed by three more factories during the same decade. Preston was arguably one of the earliest and greatest centres of the Lancashire cotton industry, where the industry was sustained from 1790 up until the mid-twentieth century.

Cotton and weaving processes were increasingly separated in the new mills of the late Victorian era and by 1850 cotton textile manufacture was the dominant trade and basis of Preston's prosperity, with around 25,000 people employed by sixty-four textile firms. The town held a leading position in spinning as well as weaving, with combined spinning and weaving

mechanisation at the forefront of the industry between 1830-80; coinciding with the apogee and decline of the twentieth-century music hall, the cotton industry reached its peak in the decade before the First World War, employing 30,000 people before the gradual onset of the industry's decline from around 1920 to the 1950s.

Commensurate with population growth the textile industry helped create a new urban industrialised working class and a six-fold increase in the population of Preston during the first half of the nineteenth century, rising from 11,887 in 1801 to 69,542 in 1851. The commercialisation and growth of music hall depended upon the amount and proportion of working-class incomes that could be spared for entertainment and drink in singing saloons and concert rooms.

The professional and clerical sector earned the highest wages. About half the population of Preston were engaged in artisan occupations and skilled workers could earn over 20s per week during good times but many were less regularly employed. There were tradesmen and shopkeepers of all kinds, including the proprietors of beerhouses and public houses, scattered around the town. Perhaps the poorest of all were the charwomen and itinerant salesmen, many of whom were almost totally destitute.

Men, women and children were engaged in cotton manufacture. Factory operatives worked up to fourteen hours a day in the early Victorian period. Legislation in 1847 (the Factory Act) and 1850 saw a reduction to a ten-and-a-half-hour day and the implementation of half-day working on Saturday. Weekly wages in the cotton industry were high relative those in other occupations: young men and women under eighteen years could earn between 5s and 13s per week. Adult women earned between 9s and 16s per week and, depending on their job description, men earned from 10 to over 20s per week.[15]

Opposite: Cotton was the staple industry in Preston throughout the Industrial Revolution. (Courtesy of the *Lancashire Evening Post*)

Right: Mrs Margaret Hindle at work in a Preston textile mill.

Preston textile workers probably had enough money to consume alcohol with their peers and workmates although their overall prosperity was affected by the periodic strikes and depressions in the industry.

The 1853 strike and lock-out lasted for nearly a year as the cotton workers tried to make up wage cuts in the 1840s. During the lock-out of 1853, Charles Dickens visited Preston and gained some inspiration for his description of Coketown in *Hard Times*. Although not intended as a literal account of Preston, there are elements in Dicken's writing signifying that the town inspired him to write about the social and topographical aspects of a town he named Coketown. The following extract from *Hard Times* describes the town and refers to the social conditions, the New Church's (present Minster) religious persuasions and the temperance influence at the height of the Industrial Revolution:

Coketown was a town of red brick, or of brick that would have been red if the smoke and ashes had allowed it; but as matters stood it was a town of unnatural red and black like the painted face of a savage. It was a town of machinery and tall chimneys, out of which interminable serpents of smoke trailed them for ever and ever, and never got uncoiled. It had a black canal in it, and a river that ran purple with ill-smelling dye, and vast piles of buildings full of windows where there was a rattling and a trembling all day long, and where the piston of the steam-engine worked monotonously up and down like the head of an elephant in a state of melancholy madness. It contained several large streets all very like one another, and many small streets still more like one another, inhabited by people equally like one another, who all went in and out at the same hours, with the same sound upon the same pavements, to do the same work, and to whom every day was the same as yesterday and tomorrow, and every year the counterpart of the last and the next ... The jail might have been the infirmary, the infirmary might have been the jail, the town hall might have been either or both... You saw nothing in Coketown but what was severely workful... If the members of a religious persuasion built a chapel there – as the members of eighteen religious persuasions had done – they made it a pious warehouse of red brick, with sometimes a bell in a birdcage on the top of it. The solitary exception was the New Church, a stuccoed edifice with a square steeple over the door, terminating in four short pinnacles like florid wooden legs. Then came the Teetotal Society, who complained that these same people would get drunk, and showed in tabular statements that they did get drunk, and proved that no inducement, human or Divine, (except a medal,) would induce them to forego their custom of getting drunk.[16]

The Victorian historian Hewitson (1883) supports the view that Preston had an exceptional level of industrial unrest: 'Numerous conflicts, some very serious, and all of them tending to weaken the bonds of mutual goodwill between the employers and the employed, have taken place in the cotton trade of Preston.' Nevertheless, between the depressions and strikes in Preston the intervening years were mainly periods of high wages and employment. The link between wage levels and the development of the pub industry is referred to by the chaplain of the House of Correction, the Revd John Clay, during the 1840s, when he attributed drunkenness to improved employment and increased wages.

The growth of Preston during the Industrial Revolution was accompanied by an increase in the number of churches and chapels. During an 1851 census of religious worship the Anglican and Catholic churches predominated in terms of numbers but Preston had the lowest overall attendance figures of any English town. Roman Catholic attendance constituted nearly half the total of worshippers in Preston and is indicative of a high native population of Roman Catholics in the town. There was also a significant Nonconformist population, about one third of Preston's Christians. It was the Nonconformist group that was to become a source of persistent opposition to music hall and a major source of the temperance movement. Joseph Livesey was born in Walton-le-Dale, Preston and was a founding member of the Preston Temperance Society. Livesey and six others introduced teetotalism to the movement through their innovation of the total abstinence pledge at Preston's first Temperance Hall on 1 September 1832. Opposition to the pub music hall, particularly from temperance campaigners, was important in shaping Preston's Victorian and Edwardian variety theatres.

During the period between 1831 and 1851 the population more than doubled to 69,542. Many men who immigrated into Preston were unable to obtain well-paid employment in the factories. One important result of this was that many families lived in primary poverty. The development of the railway network provided employment for an immigrant indigenous Irish population, which increased, from 3.3 per cent to 7.4 per cent of Preston's population in the decade following the Irish potato famine of 1840. In 1851 the total number of houses was 11,543 and each house had an average of 5.9 occupants. With this rapid growth had come the predictable sanitary and housing problems. Conditions were very cramped, frequently damp with poor hygiene standards, lighting and sanitation. Preston was without piped water, drains or sewers and the narrow passageway beyond the privy in the back yard was the place where the privy pails were emptied. Cholera and typhus were rampant and infant mortality was exceptionally high among working-class families.

The Lancashire 'Cotton Famine' (1861-1864) brought mass unemployment and poverty to Preston and extensive areas of Lancashire at the time of the American Civil War (fought

Early industrial housing, Mount Pleasant Street, Preston, 1952. (Courtesy of Harris Reference Library, Preston)

between 1861-1865). Charles Dickens showed empathy with the workforce when he addressed the cotton workers of the town in 1861 and gave readings from *A Christmas Carol* and *The Pickwick Papers* at the Corn Exchange, but with seats ranging from 1s to 4s the town was hardly living up to *Great Expectations*. Historians have debated the extent to which the depression was caused by the North's blockade of southern shipping or whether the war masked an impending cyclical trade depression; a commercial crisis on this scale had profound economic and social implications for Preston, particularly as many of the working class were, in effect, reduced to pauperism.

Below the surface there was still plenty to shock in the immediate post-famine period with miscreants, prostitutes and vagrants indulging in both petty and serious crime. Indeed the conditions in Victorian Preston were deplorable. Judging by a February 1865 report in *The Preston Chronicle*, had Charles Dickens visited the local thief's kitchen he would probably have encountered the Preston equivalent of Oliver Twist:

Congregations of all sorts of men, women and children are gathered in the thief's kitchen. In all of them there are scales with which the proprietor weighs the bread begged by the tramps during the day, before he purchases it. In these places lads, women, men, girls, beggars, thieves, tramps, vagabonds, cripples and prostitutes sleep together, without any respect to age or any distinction of sex, huddling in imperfectly ventilated rooms, and taking off their clothing before retiring to rest on account of the vermin.

The report concluded with the remark: 'As to the houses of ill fame, we have no new remedy to suggest. There were twenty-seven lodging houses of receivers of stolen goods, thirty-one public houses, twenty-five beerhouses, two coffee shops, and six suspected houses all of which are known resorts of thieves and prostitutes and sixty-one brothels.'

Prostitutes used certain music halls for business and an alarmingly high number of young girls in Victorian Preston (1865) were described as *filles publiques*, and frequented the streets and music-hall taverns:

Is it not possible for a man to walk the distance between the Parish Church and the Theatre Royal, without being accosted and stopped by numbers of girls many of them of an age in which, in ordinary life a girl is considered a child. The area of the Orchard and Friargate is infested by bonnet-less young girls... Something ought to be done about the 120 women and girls known to the police as being on the streets of Preston... there are scores of children on the streets of Preston.

The evidence contained in social nuggets of long ago also demonstrates that the social conditions in Victorian Preston could hardly equate with the 'good old days'. Vitriolic newspaper columnists challenged the existence of music halls by attacking them as places of abject poverty, inebriation, vice and crime and all frequented by young men and women. A *Chronicle* correspondent in 1865 wrote:

On a Saturday evening we set out with the intention of visiting a few of the cheap hops of which in Preston there are many... The second singing room we visited was up a flight of steps out of a stable yard, in a court not a hundred miles from the market place... Can any good emanate from such places... Little by little the girl loses her modesty, and the end is as sure and certain as is the clergyman's hope of her joyful resurrection after her life of vice with its daily battling with hunger, and her wretched death in the workhouse infirmary.

The prospect of incarceration in the one of the town's parish workhouses or in the single union workhouse in Watling Street Road, first established in 1868, was a daunting one. In the above passage the girl's 'wretched death in the workhouse infirmary,' epitomises tragic stories of sadness and misfortune that are sometimes told about workhouse inmates. In May 1864, the *Chronicle* emphasised the deterrent effect of the proposed new building. 'One large workhouse would have more of a deterrent effect than the honey-suckle fronted places we now have. It would be a bigger and more tremendous embodiment of pauperism – that repulsive idea that we associate with workhouses would be more tangible.'

The punishment of offenders was, for some, regarded as just another attraction in Preston. The principal whipping was done at a pump near the Wagon and Horses, at the top of Lord Street. Hewitson recalled that, 'enthusiastic blacksmiths, working in shops used to run out when whipping commenced, with pieces of iron, and apply them with much vigour to the backs of individuals passing through their initiatory flogging.' Rogues who had been flogged in the Market Square were taken to the Swan Inn, the White Bull and the Golden Ball public houses, not for a gin or beer, but to have their wounds washed in rum or salt water! The ultimate deterrent was also a public spectacle, though unfortunately the staged executions were not quite so quick as the dropping of the tabs at the local George Concert Hall. During the same week the George opened in November 1864, public executions were still being carried out under the gaze of the public during a period when there were moves afoot to abolish publish executions.

The above scenes were hardly consistent with the allegory of the good old days of the mid-1860s. Nevertheless, the popular entertainment and music-hall industry was such a

Preston Public Hall. The frontage has been preserved and converted into a public house but the auditorium has been demolished. (Courtesy of the *Lancashire Evening Post*)

significant part of working-class culture that, despite the severe economic hardship that resulted from the peak of the Cotton Famine in around 1863, the working classes sustained their interest in popular culture, public houses and the associated commercial music-hall industry in Preston, though there was undoubtedly scope for social and economic reform.

The opening of the town hall incorporating the Guild Hall in 1867 provided audience capacity for 1,000 patrons, and was a venue for public meetings, balls, and concert recitals. In 1882 the original Corn Exchange was extended and rebuilt as the public hall, a venue for public meetings, exhibitions and musical entertainment. With capacity for 3,500 people, it was one of the largest public halls in Lancashire and together with improved transport systems enhanced the social life of the town.

Railway beginnings coincide with the emergence of singing saloons, circus and theatre. The start of the complete railway system in the Preston area came with the opening of the Wigan to Preston Railway, later the North Union Railway, on 1 November 1838. Hewitson did not speak too favourably about the original North Union Preston railway station or the railway engines: 'At Preston the station was one of the most dismal, dilapidated, disgraceful-looking structures in Christendom... the weak character of the old engines was such that often, when a heavy train was leaving Preston for the north, porters had to push at the side by way of assistance.'

Following the opening of the Wigan to Preston Railway in 1838, Preston soon had transport links with London and circus and theatre featured international performances on a lavish scale, increasingly served by the railway with improved mobility for scenery, animals, equipment and of course, performers and audiences.

The first excursions at holiday time were advertised as providing new delights of travel for passengers on the horse-drawn trains from Preston, Grimsargh and Longridge.

An aerial view of Preston in the 1930s, featuring the Harris Museum and Art Gallery (centre), the Gothic town hall and three extant theatres. (Courtesy of the *Lancashire Evening Post*)

Three hundred and fifty-seven passengers were conveyed on the newly opened Preston to Longridge Railway, with four trains despatched each way to explore the fells and quarries of Longridge, and the good folk had a chance to witness the festivities of Preston on Whit Monday. This included the Friendly Societies paraded in the mornings and the Temperance Society paraded in the afternoon, and both with bands of music. In the thronged streets, itinerant musicians from a blind fiddler attended only by his dog, to a complete band of first-rate performers were exerting themselves to the seekers of pleasure.

The cultural and social interests of rural villagers at Longridge and other communities along the line were now to be fulfilled with train excursions to Preston's travelling circus and menageries, theatres and the very first singing saloons and free-and-easy entertainment staged in public houses. Into the bargain of cheap travel the rural community could witness the first brass bands by around 1840 as well as witness the temperance processions or seek advice from the Friendly Societies that met in pubs and would often be available to negotiate funds for sickness and unemployment.

By the late 1840s those factory workers who wanted to 'be besides the seaside' could board a train from the cotton towns to Fleetwood with cheap Sunday excursions departing Preston at 7.40 a.m. and arriving at Fleetwood at 9 a.m. The more unwavering passengers were probably induced by the

A 1930s view of Friargate, Preston, taken from the roof of the Harris Museum and Art Gallery. (Courtesy of Harris Reference Library, Preston)

prospect of bathing in the sea before going to church. 'Parties availing themselves of these trains, will be enabled to bathe and refresh themselves in ample time to attend a place of worship.'

During the latter half of the nineteenth century the high rate of population growth receded and the social climate of the town improved with less overcrowding, higher wages and an improved standard of living for a population of 112,989 by 1901. Walton argues that, in Lancashire, 'Substantial increases in cotton workers' wages are not in evidence until after the Cotton Famine. The mid-Victorian period sees little gains in real wages, punctuated by severe economic crises and accompanied by persisting low standards of health and hygiene'.[17] Widespread improvement of the Lancashire economy followed a wages boom in the early 1870s with improved housing, municipal amenities and a reduction of disease and premature death. During 1877 the chief constable of Preston reflected on the level of increased prosperity of textile workers: 'They earn pretty fair wages and as a rule they spend pretty freely. A man receives his wages on a Friday and generally he will spend a portion of those in drink before he gets home.'

In Preston, extensive improvements and slum-clearance programmes were introduced with the Bye Laws of 1876 and the Preston Improvement Act of 1880. Morgan confirms: 'Preston's housing was revolutionised with this legislation with most new housing good enough to survive until the present day.' The opening of the Gaiety Music Hall in 1882 was part of the process of urban enrichment taking place in the latter part of the nineteenth century, when Preston's commerce, business, and industrial fabric underwent considerable expansion. Hewitson refers to the very real advances made by the time of the Preston Guild (1882) in the social and physical fabric of the town.

New industries were founded when W. Dick and J. Kerr established engineering works in 1897 to meet the growing demand for tramcars and railway locomotives. This became one of the town's major twentieth-century employers employing over 10 per cent of the male workers of the town, compared to 23 per cent working in all branches of cotton. At the same time, the textile industry remained important for the town's economy and was still employing 30,000 people in 1911. Preston Docks was opened for commercial trading during 1892, providing about 500 jobs by 1911.

The depression was felt between 1929 and 1933 and saw unemployment in the town of between 5-10,000 workers. Social stability featured high in the minds of those aspiring to positions of authority and theatre and cinema had a part to play in those depressed years. In May 1929 the mayor of Preston spoke of the influence of entertainment in the *Lancashire Daily Post*: 'It is my opinion and I think it is the opinion of the Bench, that the proprietors of the theatres and cinemas are to be complimented for providing entertainment and keeping people off the streets.'

In consideration of the notion of 'the good old days' in Preston, this preamble has alluded to squalor, poverty, crime, and low moral standards, and the overall hypothesis put forward is that there can be no justification whatever for any pre-conceived literal interpretation of 'the good old days' having any truth in Victorian Preston.

Accolade: A Gallery View of Victorian Preston Featuring
The Watercolours of Edwin Beattie (1845-1917)

Lea's Virgin Inn, Anchor Weind (1894).

Starch House Square later became a bus station before it was demolished in the 1960s to make way for the town's inner ring road.

Site of the Miller Arcade, Church Street, *c.* 1850.

Cheapside, Market Square and town hall. In the foreground is the reinstated obelisk.

The 1782 town hall and (left) Guild Hall, Church Street. On the right is the present Minster.

The Starch Houses viewed from High Street (1891), hence 'Starch House Square', remembered by older generations of Prestonians.

Above is the Old Shambles and the Shoulder of Mutton pub. Alongside is 'Gin Bow entry' (1882); Preston parish church is below.

Above: Lang's Swan With Two Necks, Straight Shambles (1882), before the site was occupied by the Harris Museum and Art Gallery.

Following page: 'Doing the Academy' with the Great Vance – see page 44 for more. details (Courtesy P. Vickers)

DOING THE ACADEMY.

SUNG BY THE
GREAT VANCE.

Scene One: Early Leisure Forms and Curtain Up at the Theatre Royal

The construction of the music-hall set prompts analysis of the range of popular cultural activity that preceded music hall and was contemporaneous with it. Music-hall programming consisted of elements embracing circus numbers, music and theatre and innovations such as the bioscope. These were derived from travelling players, street ballad singers, assembly rooms, pleasure gardens, circus and the travelling fairs and menageries offering side-shows, novelties, roundabouts, peep shows and primitive projection equipment.

Preston is especially famous for its Guild Merchant conferred by ancient charter in 1179 by Henry II. 'Once every Preston Guild,' is a local expression meaning 'once every twenty years.' The historic Guild Merchant was first recognised in a charter drawn up by the town's burgesses in 1179 but it was only after 1542 that the twenty-year cycle was adopted. The sequence of Guilds has only been interrupted once in 1942 because of wartime hostilities. It is the town's greatest indoor and outdoor extravaganza with events including the historic Guild Court, inter-denominational Church and trade processions, and culminating in a Saturday night torchlight procession and varied entertainment to suit all tastes.

'To be or not to be [in Preston], that is the question' – did William Shakespeare stay in Lancashire at Hoghton Tower, six miles to the east of Preston and still the ancestral home of the De Hoghton family? There are certain enigmas in the surviving traces of the bard's teenage years, but overall the evidence amongst leading academic historians supports the theory that he did reside there, and at other Lancashire noblemen's houses during the Renaissance. William's father John had signed a pledge of faith to the English Catholics, and the presumption of William's Catholicism is no new theory. Shakespeare is said to have used the alias

The 1972 Preston Guild showing the Trade Procession on Friargate (looking towards the city centre).

Above: The 1972 Preston Guild Trade Procession, Friargate.

Below: The Public Hall hosted the opening of the Guild Court on Monday 1 September 1952. (Courtesy of the *Lancashire Evening Post*)

William Shakeshafte whilst enjoying the charismatic company of Priest Edmund Campion, which probably explains why he used the alias.[18] 'To be or not to be' – time to reflect on Hamlet's famous soliloquy. Nevertheless Preston was the scene of many performances by strolling players who enlivened the fairs and festivals throughout the Middle Ages. Players would arrive with ceremonial fanfares and descend on inns and warehouses, or perform in the open air.

Long before the growth of the music-hall industry, provincial permanent theatres were rare in the eighteenth century, and in northern England the Grand Theatre at Lancaster and the Georgian Theatre at Richmond survive as two of the oldest theatres in the country. The first reference to a theatre in Preston was made by Thomas Bellingham, who wrote in his diary on the 16 August 1688: 'Att night, I saw a farce called ye devil and Ye Pope.' In Lang's map of Preston, published in 1744, the earliest theatre is shown as being situated in Woodcock's Court, off Fishergate.

General Burgoyne was on stage here in 1771 when he spoke on behalf of the charities of Preston. This was the original playhouse and a playbill shows that in May 1796 the 'theatre' was presenting a drama, *The Earl of Essex,* with Mr and Mrs Phelps playing the respective parts of Sir Walter Raleigh and Queen Elizabeth. There was also a musical interlude with a song by Mr and Miss Goldfinch and a very early pantomime – *The birth and adventures of Harlequin*; the celebrated pantomime as originally performed at the Theatre Royal, Drury Lane, London.' The pantomime featured 'a farm yard at sun rising with an incantation of the witches and the birth of Harlequin from an egg.'

This incidental pantomime, staged during May at the beginning of Preston's Industrial Revolution, would have been attended by adults of all social classes, demonstrating that the earliest pantomimes were not the type presented as Christmas entertainment for children.

Joseph Grimbaldi is credited with establishing pantomime as a British entertainment at Covent Garden in 1806. Perhaps because of its rich historical past, pantomime is packed with traditions and superstitions handed down from generation to generation and was certainly an influence in the music hall with integrated song and comedy acts forming the basis of the music-hall repertoire. Pantomime developed in the Victorian theatres of Preston into a bulging Christmas cracker of family entertainment. Little had changed by the Edwardian period, for the annual pantomime remained a holiday music hall in disguise, a spectacle for parents as much as their children. It was all a rout of dames, demon kings, cats and brokers' men, babes and barons, chorus songs, haunted bedrooms, and men dressed up as cows, and so it remains. Indeed, Preston has produced two of the greatest and best-loved pantomime dames, namely John Inman and Roy Barraclough.

Circus was originally an invention of Philip Astley in the late 1760s. The number of circuses and menageries visiting Preston during the first half of the nineteenth-century began to make an impact on audiences. Legendary nomadic showmen including Wombwell and Atkins with a procession of traction engines, trailers and animals brought the circus and menageries to a curious Preston public who had never seen exotic animals such as lions from far-off lands. At one time George Wombwell owned more than twenty lions and five elephants.

This type of entertainment seems to have been popular across the social strata with admission prices ranging between 6d and 1s for an 1824 travelling menagerie and fair featuring lions and wild animals. Atkins' Royal Menagerie visited the market place on the 27 March, 1824. The propaganda in *The Preston Chronicle* reported on what sounded like the equivalent of Blackpool's Golden Mile:

> There were extraordinary scenes of affection for the performing male lion and the beautiful
> Bengal tigress in the same cage. The noble lioness has again whelped two cubs – the cubs,

All the fun of the travelling fair. (Drawing by C. Dodding)

which are now living in perfect health, are so tame and inoffensive that they may be handled and caressed with the same ease and safety as a lap dog. And as for that truly singular and most wonderful animal, the Aurochos – words can only convey the two long horns growing from its forehead in a form peculiar to no other animal – See a pair of those extraordinary rare birds, the pelicans of the wilderness – the only two in the United Kingdoms.

During the Preston Guild of August 1842, 'Pablo Fanque's Circus Royal' visited Preston. The admission prices during Guild Week were doubled for a superior company of male and female equestrians, the diminutive fairy ponies, (Albert and Nelson) and ropedancers. Management claimed the 'first female equestrians in the world'. Following the Guild, the circus reopened and the public of Preston were given the opportunity to see the circus at the old prices of front boxes 2s, side boxes 1s, pit 6d, and gallery 3d – prices that would still have been unaffordable for many in 1842.

The more affluent were conveyed in sedan chairs to balls and private parties at the assembly rooms at the Bull Hotel, Church Street. Whittle (1821) described:

the elegant and remarkable capacious room, built at the sole expense of the Earl of Derby, is situated down the court of the Bull Inn. It is embellished by three grand glass chandeliers, which dazzle the eyes of the beholder at first sight… there is an attic orchestra at the head of the room and balls are held here.[19]

The Coronation of George IV was celebrated in fine style at the assembly rooms: on the 14 October 1821, 'The ladies and gentlemen of Preston and its vicinity are respectfully informed that there will be a ball and supper at the assembly room in honour of the Coronation of George IV. Dancing to commence at eight o'clock, ladies 5/, and gentlemen 5/-.'

The genteel set enjoyed therapeutic activities in the first established clubs of Preston exemplified by the curiously named 'Preston Oyster and Parched Pea Club'. This was established in 1773 and continued until 1841 with weekly meetings often held at the old Mitre Inn, Fishergate. The chief business of the members consisted of wine drinking and the devouring oysters interspersed with music and poetry. The hierarchal officers of the club comprised an officer they called 'Oystericus,' whose main duty was to order the oysters which arrived every week from London, while 'Cellarius,' provided port of the finest quality.

The Preston Catch and Glee Club was first established in 1819 with a weekly winter syllabus of refined cultural activities and musical evenings such as a choir performing 'The Chough and the Crow' in September 1835. Some aristocratic members of these clubs would have made up the audience at the Theatre Royal, which summoned the attendance of the nobility and gentry at the beginning of Preston's Industrial Revolution.

During the years 1802-1982 a place of entertainment stood at the corner of Fishergate and Theatre Street and during over 180 years of entertainment it played host to countless legendary names of stage and screen. We will see that one former owner, Mr Parkinson, resisted the temptation to turn the theatre into a full-time music hall and that may have been its downfall.

Originally the historic theatre was built by a body of shareholders and its opening coincided with the Preston Guild in 1802. Fifteen transferable silver tickets were issued to shareholders of the Theatre Royal on 16 January 1805 to enable the bearer to gain free admission to the performances. The silver medallion was about the size of the old 5s piece bearing the head of Shakespeare, with the inscription, 'We shall not look on his like again'. The reverse side had the inscription 'Preston Theatre' and the number and initials of the bearer.

Opening productions in August 1802 included a balance of musical drama, farce, and Shakespeare. Mr And Mrs Siddons demonstrated their versatility by each playing several parts, including Mr Siddon playing Hamlet and Mrs Siddons playing Ophelia in the same production. The theatre was fairly typical of the era and in later years was described as being 'the most important historic place of amusement in Preston.' Little is known about the structure or audience capacity of the original theatre, although a watercolour in the Harris Art Gallery shows the theatre as a curious barn-like structure with a loft door with hoists above, and the entrance doors indicating 'pit', 'gallery' and 'boxes' below.

The Preston historian Whittle described the theatre in 1821:

> The town can boast of having an extensive theatre, very commodious, and well fitted for the purposes of the drama; inside consists of two tiers of boxes on each side, the pit and the gallery are capacious, the scenery is good and the whole house well ornamented but as yet the gas has yet to be introduced; the stage is spacious, and well adapted to convey the voice intelligibly to the ear; the boxes are tastefully decorated, and well arranged for the accommodation of the numerous visitors who frequent it during the race week, and other seasons of the year. It is hoped that this place will be resorted to during the ensuing Guild Year, 1822, by those ladies and gentlemen visiting the town during this grand fête; no doubt able performers will be brought down from the metropolis, for the purpose of giving éclat to this festival, celebrated every twentieth year.

At the time of the opening of the Theatre Royal in 1802, and during the first quarter of the nineteenth century, Preston was still dominated by lawyers, doctors, merchants, shopkeepers and bankers and increasingly, wealthy mill owners. The Theatre Royal with its bourgeois and aristocratic elements of the society of the nineteenth century enjoyed concert recitals, dramatic productions and Shakespeare's plays including *King Lear* and *Romeo and Juliet* presented at the theatre during July and September 1825.

This Present FRIDAY.

NEW THEATRE, PRESTON

On FRIDAY, AUGUST 27th, 1802,

THE MUSICAL DRAMA OF THE

Mountaineers

Octavian, Mr. *SIDDONS*
Bulcazem Muley, Mr. REMINGTON
Count Virolet, Mr. BANNERMAN
Killmallock, Mr. NICHOLSON——Lope Toche, Mr. HAYES
Roque, Mr. DAWSON
Muleteers and Goatherds, Mr. NEWTON, Mr. MASON, and Mr. FROST
Sadi, Mr. CRISP
Floranthe, Mrs. *H. SIDDONS*
Zoriada, Mrs. CUMMINS
Agnes, Mrs. CRISP
Female Goatherds, Mrs. ROWLAND, Mrs. NICHOLSON,
Mrs. and Miss REMINGTON

A Comic SONG, by Mr. NEWTON,
And a Favorite SONG, by Mrs. ROWLAND.

After which, a celebrated FARCE, (never performed here) called The

Wedding Day;
Or the Meeting of Old Friends.

Sir Adam Contest, Mr. CRISP
Lord Rakeland, Mr. BANNERMAN
Young Contest, Mr. MASON
Mr. Milden, Mr. FROST——John, Mr. NEWTON
Lady Contest, Mrs. CRISP
With the favorite Song of " IN THE DEAD OF THE NIGHT."
Lady Autumn, Mrs. NICHOLSON
Hannah, Miss REMINGTON
Mrs. Hamford, Mrs. REMINGTON

An entire new Comic Song, called, The ASSIZES, by Mr. CRISP.

TICKETS to be had, and PLACES for the BOXES taken at Mrs. SERGENT's *(only)*
Printer, MARKET-PLACE.
BOXES 3s.......PIT 2s.......GALLERY 1s.
DOORS to be Opened at SIX, and to Begin at SEVEN o'Clock precisely.

On SATURDAY, the Tragedy of HAMLET.
Hamlet, Mr. SIDDONS......Ophelia, Mrs. H. SIDDONS
With LOVERS' QUARRELS.

Left: Playbill of the Theatre Royal, Preston, dated 27 August 1802. (Courtesy of the *Lancashire Evening Post*)

Below: Theatre Royal, Preston, 1802. (Drawing by C. Dodding)

Theatre Royal. Preston.

During the pre-Victorian era admission prices at the Preston theatre were generally high for the range of eclectic programming that was often proclaimed for the attention of the nobility and gentry. Class differences and the patronage of fashionable society at plays and opera brought about changes in the seating of the theatre. The performances at the Theatre Royal usually commenced at 7 p.m. and were divided into three parts, presenting quasi-dramatic productions, musical interludes, farce, singing, circus and comic routines. Lengthy performances prevented the factory operatives and many apprentices from attending a full performance although cheaper seats in the gallery were offered after 9 p.m.

Preston audiences bore some relationship to the social scale of the particular theatre or music-hall venue. Originally audiences at the theatre contrasted greatly with the original public house taverns such as the Albion, offering the first free-and-easy music-hall acts. Notwithstanding a pretentious class gulf, philanthropic interests were served at the theatre during August 1826 when the manager allocated a night for the benefit of the poor.

> The manager most respectfully intimates to the public, that impressed with sentiment and warmest gratitude for the liberal support he has so invariably received from the inhabitants of Preston, to propose benefit for the distressed operatives of this town. Friday is the evening appointed for the above purpose, which it is hoped will be met with that support Preston has so frequently bestowed.

Many provincial towns had their own resident stock company which was often enhanced by leading actors from London who travelled from town to town playing their famous parts with the local company:

> On the 18th July, 1825 Miss Clara Fisher, direct from the Theatre Royal, Drury Lane, London, played the part of 'Goldfinch,' in the comedy, 'The Road to Ruin,' at Preston and Mr J. Crisp performed 'Crack,' in the musical farce of the 'Turnpike Gate,' as originally acted by him in Preston, and London.

Whittle (1821) was condemnatory of the earliest dramatic production at the theatre suggesting a moralistic stance: 'Drama never flourished to any great extent in Preston. To people of morose and narrow minds, who viewed theatrical performances as abuses that ought to be expelled from society as tending to feed the passions, and thereby nursing vice.'

Nevertheless, pantomime enjoyed wider public appeal and featured at the Theatre Royal during December 1825 with, 'the grand eastern dramatic spectacle of "Aladdin or the Wonderful Lamp." The Theatre Royal had an important role to play in pantomime as well as circus development, with the theatre integrating comedy and circus entertainment as comic intervals into dramatic performances. During 1829, a performance at the theatre presented a comic-inspired circus interval between two plays, featuring two men, Jocko and Jacko, masquerading as monkeys around the gallery and upper boxes, before carrying out a daring circus escapade from gallery to stage. This is an example of the kind of act that was later incorporated into music-hall programmes and perhaps illustrates how audiences was being drawn towards the culture of music hall, albeit, in this instance, in the established theatre.

During 1833, extensive renovations to the theatre were implemented by a former London theatre manager Watkin Burroughs, who took over as manager and attempted to raise the tone of the theatre by increasing admission prices: 'To put the theatre in a proper state to receive the first classes of society, the manager submits the following prices to the public – boxes 2/6d, pit 1s/6d, gallery 6d.' These prices illustrate segregation of working-class audiences; indeed, in 1833, the purchase of even a gallery seat at sixpence would have been unaffordable for many textile workers. It is conceivable that class prejudice in the theatre may have assisted the growth of provincial music hall where cheap drink was copiously supplied. A total abstinence pledge had originated in Preston less than twelve months before Watkin took office and he was anxious to upgrade the theatre and attract the upper strata of society for whom perfect sobriety mattered by assuring patrons that:

> The theatre interior has been splendidly embellished and the scenery entirely repainted. At a time when all classes are so earnestly exhorted to temperance, the manager trusts it will not be irrelevant to state that a theatrical performance affords a highly rational evening's amusement and the visitor leaves the theatre frequently morally improved and certainly without any exposure to inebriety as no spirits or wines can be obtained even if desired.

The teetotal movement was expressed nine years later with the staging of the propagandist play *The Trial of John Barleycorn* at the Theatre Royal in 1842.

Before the opening of the town hall in 1867 and the converted public hall in 1853, the Theatre Royal fulfilled the role of both theatre and multi-purpose hall for meetings and functions governing the public and social life of Preston. The internationally famed Preston astronomer Moses Holden presented a triennial series of lectures here from 1815 to 1852. They were illustrated with 'the most beautiful geastrodianphanic or grand transparent orrery, twenty four feet in diameter, with superb scenery; of the sun, moon, planets, and stars, shining as they do in nature, enlightening all the place.'

Astronomical innovation aside, it now seems beyond belief that on the site of a modern retail store in Preston's Fishergate, great exponents of culture, including such names as Franz Lizst and Niccolò Paganini, had delighted audiences during the first half of the nineteenth century. 'Signor Paganini is mentioned in Whittle's *History of Preston* as giving a great performance in the Theatre Royal on the 27th August 1833; performing before the nobility and gentry and inhabitants of Preston previous to his departure to the Court of St Petersburg.'

Admission prices targeted the aristocracy, ranging from box (7s 6d), and pit (5s) to gallery (3s), and drew a large audience, according to *The Preston Chronicle*:

> The wonderful violinist gave his promised concert at the theatre on Tuesday evening last, to a crowded and fashionable audience who testified their admiration of his extraordinary musical powers by loud and enthusiastic plaudits at every pause in his performance... On one or two occasions during the evening, the signor appeared to have succeeded in some new and brilliant extempore passage, and expressed his own satisfaction by smiles approaching to laughter, amidst the simultaneous, deafening, and repeated cheers of the house.

The great Hungarian-born composer and performer Franz Lizst trod the same boards as the virtuoso violinist when he graced the stage of the Theatre Royal on Wednesday 2 December 1840. Lizst toured extensively in Europe and gave concerts for charitable purposes. During 1840-41 he made further visits to England, playing before Queen Victoria; in December 1840 he played at five north-west venues, in Halifax, Liverpool, Manchester, Rochdale and Preston. Lizst would normally have received the kind of adulation now reserved for leading pop musicians and groups, but at Preston they did not even have to find the 'house full' sign:

> There was a fair sprinkling of the fashionable and respectable of the town. It would have been gratifying, however, on such an occasion, had every part of the house been occupied to

A portrait of Franz Lizst, who gave a recital at the Theatre Royal in December 1840. (Musée Carnavalet, Paris)

repletion… Notwithstanding the immense merit of Lizst and despite his European reputation he had so readily acquired the Preston Concert was by no means worthy of the musical reputation of Preston or commensurate with his high deserts.

We note a sprinkling of the fashionable and respectable, or perhaps more specifically, provincial, gentry. Spring 1846 saw the high standards perpetuated with another change of manager. The *Preston Guardian* reported that:

> The edifice has undergone a complete renovation, and received every attention that can possibly promote the comfort of the audience and actors, and the cleanliness and warmth of the house… As we announced last week the theatre will be opened on the 20th July, under the sole management of Chas James, a former lessee of the Queen's Theatre, London. The high character and respectability of this gentleman and the talent of the company, together with the great resources of his London establishment in scenery, and wardrobe induce us to expect that the re-opening will surpass anything yet exhibited on these boards.

In January 1848, quite early in the growth of Preston's music-hall industry, the Theatre Royal featured a group of 'American Serenaders'. The respectable audience was said to consist of all classes who shared an association between singer and song and were invited to participate in the performance by buying the songbook – an important feature of the culture of later music hall. 'Introducing their favourite and popular overtures, glees and songs, accompanied with banjos, bones and triangles…The taste for melodies in this town must be very great for on Monday evening every part of the house was crowded and hundreds, it is said, went away unable to gain admittance.' The success of this 1848 performance, together with the pantomime performances, suggests the theatre was rivalling the growing music-hall industry in the town.

On the 14 September 1861 the famous tightrope walker 'Blondin' starred at the Theatre Royal, illustrating the ongoing popularity of circus performers throughout the nineteenth century. During the same year, coinciding with the beginning of the Cotton Famine, a visitor to Preston described the popularity of the pit and gallery with audiences at the Theatre Royal: 'The audience composed of factory operatives, occupied the pit and gallery, and brought their babies with them.' The lower priced tickets were in the gallery, gods and the pit; the latter situated behind the front stalls. The gallery was segregated in most theatres and music halls by a separate entrance at the side of the building where the gallery audience had to endure the rigours of many steps and hard bench seats without back rests. The gallery and the pit were the preserve of young working-class men and women of various ages, though on this occasion the young women may have ignored the frequent notices that 'Children in arms will not be admitted.'

The same visitor admired the lavish auditorium:

The red lamps that light up the portico, induced us to make, in the evening, an examination of it from within... the ceiling is divided into eight compartments, radiating from a sun-burner in the centre, with a figure disporting in each compartment. The boxes over the proscenium are hung with bed curtains, and look quite as much like berths on board a ship: and the decorations generally are in what might be called the paperhanging style.

On the theme of the marine environment a certain local fishmonger, Professor Robert Blezard, describing himself as a 'Professor of Oysters', attempted to educate his audience on the curiosities of the deep but successfully managed to plunge the theatre into utter chaos during an 1862 unscripted presentation on how to devour the oyster with aplomb. The house was in uproar with plenty of jeering and spontaneous comment from high in the gods but recorded for posterity as an amusing anecdote of the social history of Preston and its theatre:

The doors were open at half past seven and there was a considerable rush at first into the gallery. The house was filled as follows: pit about three-fourths, gallery, three fourths, upper boxes one fourth and boxes about one half. The fish dealing division had mustered in strong force and there were several women present... Mr Blezard was dressed in a black coat, trousers, and vest and white gloves. Taking off his hat he bowed to the assembly – 'Ladies and gentlemen (laughter and cheers) I thank you for your kind encouragement and support. I must say ladies and gentlemen I have not quite as full a house as I expected; therefore I must keep my courage up. I must say that this ere is the finest thing that ever came before you. Therefore there is no telling what this lecter will do!'

Robert advanced to the footlights and raised his left hand to the gallery as if to procure order. He said, 'Now there is great talk about Shakespeare. I can tell you one thing that Shakespeare got all his studies off... [a voice shouted 'tripe Bob']... no, off oyster suppers.' In the same strain he proceeded to recommend the best drinks after oyster – whisky or porter for those who were not teetotal and warm milk for those who were.

Robert was met by a storm of hisses and uncomplimentary expression. A scuffle ensued for the barrels of oysters placed on the stage, in the course of which paraffin lamps were knocked over into the orchestra where the scuffle continued. During the evening two potatoes and an egg were thrown at the lecturer in a manner befitting the infamous Glasgow Empire, where disgruntled patrons sometimes threw tomatoes at the performer or observed long periods of silence if they did not like the comedian. Remarkably, the Professor and Mrs Blezard regarded the evening as a triumphant success, 'especially in a business point of view.'

AN ACCOUNT OF THE

GRAND OYSTER DEMONSTRATION

AT THE

THEATRE ROYAL, PRESTON,

AND THE CELEBRATED

ORATION

BY PROFESSOR BLEZARD.

COMICAL SCENES, AND DESPERATE RALLY FOR EIGHT BARRELS OF OYSTERS AT THE CONCLUSION.

ALSO

OYSTERS:

THEIR NUTRITIOUS AND MEDICINAL QUALITIES;

AND

FAMILIAR CHAT CONCERNING OYSTERS.

COMPILED FROM EMINENT AUTHORITIES

BY PROFESSOR BLEZARD,

OYSTER MERCHANT, PRESTON.

PRICE THREEPENCE.

The front cover of the *Preston Mercury*, 1862, depicting Professor Blezard's performance with the oysters.

Following the chaos of this particular Lancashire dissipation and a potential disaster with the paraffin lamps the theatre was not burnt down. Nevertheless there were eighty-seven instances of theatre fires in the United Kingdom between 1850 and 1900. Preston duly made its mark with instances of theatre fires at the Theatre Royal (1884) and a serious fire at the Prince's Theatre (1900).

The *Preston Guardian's* report of the 1 March 1884 on the fire at the Theatre Royal makes interesting reading, but it was no musical hall joke!

At 2.30 a.m., Thursday last a fire was discovered to have broken out at the Theatre Royal. Thomas Pearson, the postman in charge of the small cart was returning from the railway station when he noticed signs of burning coming from the theatre. He drove onto Lune Street and alerted two policemen who went to the stage door where the fire was discernible. They at once blew their whistles and together with four more policemen they used a plank as a battering ram to break down the door. The whole of the stage nearest to Theatre Street was enveloped in flames. The fire brigade attended and, together with the police using buckets of water, the fire was extinguished. One end of the stage together with the proscenium and one of the boxes was burnt. Scenery, stage furniture and properties were completely destroyed. The Manager, Mr Ramsay attended and estimated it would be at least a fortnight before theatrical performances could resume.

Voice From the Gods

'For the benefit of our patrons ices and fruit crush will be served during the intervals at each performance.'

Scene Two: Rivals in Leisure: The Theatre Royal Versus Music Hall

In Preston and elsewhere there was increasing competition from rival concert halls to the established theatre during the second half of the nineteenth century:

> The theatre is the most popular resort of pleasure-seeking workmen and the gallery their favourite part of the house… After the theatres the music halls are the most popular places of Saturday night resort with working men and in them they can combine the drinking of the Saturday night glass and the smoking of the Saturday night pipe with the seeing and hearing of a variety of entertainments.[20]

Preston Theatre Royal developed its response to music halls to such an extent that the working classes were able to consider theatre and music-hall entertainment as direct alternatives particularly as its stage witnessed a pantomime appearance of one of the most famous stars of the Victorian music hall, albeit at the beginning of his career as a circuit actor:

'The Great Vance' in Preston

Albert Vance or 'The Great Vance,' as he was known, was part of a group known as the 'Lion Comiques,' who were the first great stars of the music hall. Their stage persona focused on the 'man about town', and would have been immediately recognisable by the audiences. Vance was a fashionable rake, or 'masher,' who was proud of his fair hair, and sported an eyeglass, gold-knobbed cane and jewellery, carried a gold toothpick and wore daringly tight trousers. Vance was

THEATRE ROYAL,
PRESTON.
Licensed to Mr. EDMUND FALCONER.
GREAT TREAT for the CHRISTMAS HOLIDAYS.—On Monday Evening, Dec. 26th, 1853, will be produced a Grand FAIRY EXTRAVAGANZA and COMIC PANTOMIME, entitled QUEEN MAB ! or the FAIRY OF THE LAKE OF THE SILVER SWANS and HARLEQUIN PRINCE PIPPIN, with entirely new and gorgeous Scenery, painted expressly for the occasion by Mr. W. RAMSDEN and Assistants. Extraordinary Mechanical Effects, Brilliant Costumes, Magnificent Properties, Grotesque Masks, Tricks, Traps, and Pantomimic Wonders.

The business of the Comic Scenes will be sustained by the following talented Artistes;—Clown, Mr. W. SENNETT, from the Theatres Royal Glasgow and Newcastle; Harlequin, Mr. CARLE, from the Surrey Theatre; Pantaloon, Mr. GLANVILLE, from the Theatre Royal Edinburgh; Columbine, Mrs. RAMSDEN, from the Theatre Royal, Bath; supported by a numerous and efficient CORPS DE BALLET and the whole strength of the Company.

For further particulars see Bills of the Day.

Lower Boxes, 2s.; Upper Boxes, 1s. 6d.; Pit, 9d.! Gallery, 4d. Second price at nine o'clock—Lower Boxes, 1s. 6d.; Upper Boxes, 1s.; Pit, 6d. No half-price to Gallery.

The doors will be opened at half-past six, and the performance will commence at seven o'clock precisely.

NOTE.—There will be a GRAND JUVENILE DAY PERFORMANCE of QUEEN MAB on Wednesday next, December 28th.

Preston Pilot, 24 December 1853, advertising a pantomime featuring Alfred Glanville (alias Vance) at the Theatre Royal.

CORN EXCHANGE, PRESTON.—FRIDAY & SATURDAY, May 12 and 13.

VANCE, and his Eminent CONCERT PARTY.—
Artistes: Miss MILLY HOWARD, Miss E. AMALIA, Miss E. GALTON, Mdlle. MIRIAM, and Mr. ALFRED G. VANCE.

Mr. VANCE has the honour to announce his Annual Concerts for the above dates, when an entirely new selection of Songs and Impersonations will be produced, in addition to a new Comic Operetta, entitled "Shells and Swells," in which he will sustain three distinct characters, and be supported by Miss Milly Howard, the favourite Comedienne. The entire Company will appear in a Grand Comic Festival, introducing his latest and most popular compositions.

Prices: 6d. to 3s.   Doors open 7 30 ; Overture 8 ; Carriages 10 15.

Above: Preston Guardian advertising Vance at Preston Corn Exchange during May 1871.

Right: Image of Vance. (Courtesy of P. Vickers)

born in 1839 and his real name was Alfred Peck Stevens. Using the stage name Alfred Glanville he accepted a contract of 50s per week to work in Preston under Edmund Falconer and in December 1853 he appeared as 'Pantaloon,' in the *Grand Fairy Extravaganza and Pantomime*, 'Queen Mab,' at Preston Theatre Royal. He made his debut in London at the Metropolitan in 1864, complete with monocle, and evening dress portraying the period swell, later earning £100 per week. This wealthy, upper-class, fashionable image would have probably appealed to the middle classes when he returned to Preston Corn Exchange and Guild Hall during the early 1870s but after a spectacular career in the music hall he died on stage in 1888.

The Theatre Royal Grand Music Hall

During the peak of the growth of the pub concert hall in Preston, the Theatre Royal was converted into The Theatre Royal Grand Music Hall in March 1866. The theatre had begun to feel the effects of the established concert rooms and singing saloons enticing away their working-class audiences in that it staged generic music-hall performances for three consecutive seasons between 1866-68. A capacity audience enjoyed comic vocalist, 'James Taylor, The Court Minstrels, and Dusoni Star Acrobats' and supporting cast. During 1867 a three-month season of music hall was staged in the newly dubbed 'Preston Theatre Royal Concert Hall,' and was billed as 'a grand amalgamation of star concert-hall artists selected with the greatest care from the principal London Music Halls.' A further music-hall season commenced on the 5 September 1868.[21]

The birth of music hall coincided with a sharp drop in seat prices at the theatre. Prices were designed to attract a pit or gallery working-class audience as the audience moved from class to mass audience, thus enhancing the culture with integrative social classes during its 1867 music-hall season. Prices: centre boxes 1s 6d, side boxes 1s, pit 6d, gallery 3d, (less than the cost of 6d for a gallery seat in 1833), doors open 7 p.m., to commence at 7.30 p.m., concluding 10 p.m., half price at 9 p.m., to boxes only. The management also showed a clear concern for propriety for by now the Victorian concept of respectability was being mentioned in the advertising propaganda:

> The prices of admission to be on the most reasonable terms to suit all classes of respectability; the entertainment to surpass anything yet attempted in Preston. No boys under 16 years unless accompanied by parents, Children in arms not admitted, no disorderly characters. Police officers in attendance to maintain order, three months tickets obtainable with reasonable rates from the manager.

The fifteen shareholders agreed in 1868 to sell the theatre at the rate of £286 13s 4d a share to a local operatic singer, Mr William Parkinson, of Scorton, near Preston.

During 1869, William greatly improved the theatre by adding a new frontage, which comprised shops in the basement and offices above. The façade was designed by renowned Preston architect, James Hibbert (1833-1903) who went on to design Preston's magnificent grade-one listed Harris Museum and Art Gallery, which opened in 1894. William adopted a more refined approach to programming by significantly reducing generic music-hall acts and attempting to exploit a different market for entertainment. During the first half of the 1870s the new owner/manager brought opera, pantomime and drama with higher scaled prices for operatic productions: dress circle, 3s 6d (opera 5s), side boxes 2s (opera 3s), stalls 1s 6d (opera 2s), pit 1s, gallery 6d. The former Carl Rosa Opera singer even changed the name to 'The Theatre Royal and Opera House.' On the 3 July 1872, William extolled 'much pleasure in announcing to the public of Preston that he has effected an engagement with the Rose Hersee Opera Company presenting: Wednesday - *Bohemian girl*; Thursday - *Norma*; Friday - *Faust*; Saturday - *Maritana*.

Preston Chronicle advertisement for a Theatre Royal Grand Music Hall season in 1866.

The infusion of music-hall stars in pantomime probably accustomed the family audience to variety material and persuaded more people to attend the Theatre Royal. A programme dated 21 December 1872 mentions a London pantomime with the newly installed machinery necessary for the transformation scene: *The Naughty Forty Thieves*, London pantomime with powerful company, splendid transformation scene and gorgeous dress.' This illustrates the strength of the repertoire with its technical resources and innovations. However, for the period 1869-76 there is some evidence in newspaper correspondence of a deflection of audiences from dramatic productions at the theatre to the rival attraction of the pub music hall.

Rival Attractions
In 1871 a *Chronicle* correspondent using the *nom de plume* 'Saxon' spoke of how drama was being overtaken by the popularity of the singing saloons:

> Singing or concert rooms can get crammed, while the drama gets no kind of support at all. The commercial classes and mill owners in Preston seem to have lost all taste for Shakespeare and the working classes have left *Hamlet, Macbeth* and the *Merchant of Venice* for concert rooms for Hoop di-doodem-doo, Champagne Charlie and all that kind of stupid balderdash. Men are becoming too starched or too frigid to be seen at a respectable play… To sustain proper theatrical representations men may be drawn from spending their money in drinking at concert halls hearing all sorts of blarney strung together in the shape of songs. The theatre is nearly always empty while the screaming, mocking, silly concert rooms get all the money.

Another correspondent taking a conflicting view using the pseudonym 'Live and Let Live' highlights that there was a class basis for criticism. He responded to Saxon's letter by defending the culture of the music hall and criticising the Theatre Royal on a number of counts:

> I have ceased going to the theatre for several reasons: first on account of the price; second on account of the lateness of the hour; third on account of so many lewd characters being there; and fourth on account of the talent being generally so poor. More recently I have visited a concert hall in Friargate, opposite Orchard Street, (The King's Head) and I find I can spend an hour or two any evening, between 7 and 10 o'clock, for about 3d or 4d and really enjoy myself by listening to stupid balderdash such as our friend 'Saxon' appears to have got so thoroughly disgusted with. By hearing first-class songs by first-class artistes I consider myself as particular as any one, in my choice of entertainment. I have neither heard nor seen anything wrong in this place of general resort, and the only object I have in writing, is to put this concert hall business in the position it duly merits.

Saxon responded with a letter echoing rational-recreation beliefs by suggesting more cerebral activities for the working classes:

> Live and Let Live, believes in free trade amusements, but ought he not to add that he wishes the greatest success to the most instructive kinds of amusements, and that it is his duty as well as mine, to try to lift the people up into the higher, more intellectual and more virtuous amusements, especially when we can see a beautiful theatre in one of the best parts of town empty night after night.

To sum up the debate, the point made by Saxon that, 'The commercial classes and mill owners in Preston seem to have lost all taste for Shakespeare and the working classes have left *Hamlet*, *Macbeth* and the *Merchant of Venice* for concert rooms', is an interesting one. In line with their arguments there does seem to have been a definite shift away from the Theatre Royal towards music hall. The correspondence illustrates how the success of music hall aroused prejudices and how certain factions unwittingly entered the music hall versus legitimate theatre debate. The theatre had its quota of troubles and experienced mixed fortunes but during the 1870s music hall was challenging the theatre for audiences and although music hall was in serious competition with popular theatre it did not replace it. This lends support to the argument that there were prejudices towards legitimate theatre and its repertoire as certain factions transferred their allegiance to the pub concert hall at the expense of the legitimate theatre where alcohol was not so easily available.

In a letter dated 18 October 1874, William Parkinson agonised about the contest between music hall and legitimate theatre:

> If I chose to make a concert hall of the theatre I have no doubt whatever of being able to make large sums of money and at the present time when fortunes are being made in London and almost every large town in Great Britain... I object to concert halls in principle or else I could have made a fortune long ago.

Evidence of declining audiences with serious financial implications is manifest in William Parkinson's decision to sell the theatre to a local building club in 1876. Although it had not always been honey for the owners of the Theatre Royal, the venue continued as a live theatre and the ongoing appeal of all classes of pantomime, Shakespeare, melodrama and revue was sustained on this theatrical roller coaster. The new management staged one of the first revue performances in Preston on the 21 July 1878, when Mr W. Morgan gave 'a capital bill of fare – *The Three Blue Bonnets*, *Oliver Primrose* and *Stem to Stern*.'

Sir Henry Irving at The Theatre Royal – 'To be or not to be' in Preston
The Theatre Royal played host to leading actors of the time including the distinguished Shakespearean actor Henry Irving, from London's renowned Lyceum Theatre, who toured the provinces as an actor-manager with his company and visited Preston during September 1878, the events being duly reported in the *Preston Guardian*: 'Special representation of Mr Henry Irving to appear in his great representation of Hamlet, imported by the Lyceum Company, side boxes 8/-'

A review extolled the Preston performance in the national trade paper *The Era* on the 13 October 1878:

> Henry Irving and the Lyceum Theatre Company presented *Hamlet* on the first night and *The Bells*, on the second night. Mr Irving was received in a most enthusiastic manner by crowded

houses and fully retained his reputation. Called before the curtain after the last act, he was cheered to the echo. Morgan deserves the thanks of the community for affording the public of the town another chance of seeing the great actor in his choicest characters once more supported by such an excellent all round company.

The Bells, featuring Henry Irving, had rescued the ailing but now fully restored Lyceum Theatre, London for future generations and Sir Henry Irving was to become the first theatrical knight. There can be little doubt that the appearance of Sir Henry Irving was a major attraction in Preston. It is a noteworthy and perhaps unappreciated historical fact that melodrama and Shakespearian productions drew consistently good popular audiences in the period and were appreciated by both working and middle-class audiences who were prepared to pay a higher scale of admission prices of up to 8s for a box seat. *Hamlet* was played to a crowded house with a packed gallery and pit and when the evidence is weighed it becomes quite clear that to assume incomprehension on the part of the popular audience is far too simplistic; a trend not unusual in other English towns.

Reid (1980) demonstrates how Shakespeare was popular at Birmingham Theatre Royal 1845. 'A performance of *Hamlet* was played to a crowded house with a gallery crammed to suffocation and a pit no less so closely packed.' This repertoire was recognised by theatre critics as being popular with the pit and gallery audiences. The success of Preston's Theatre Royal in the presentation of prestigious and affordable Shakespearean productions in 1878 shows a parallel.

The diversity of entertainment in Preston was represented on the 2 October 1880, with a dioramic season presented by H. Hamilton. The scenes represented were from the Zulu and Afghan wars:

> Impressionist Miss Helen Heffer. The OICM Minstrels, Band. Private Box £1, 2/-, 1/- and 6d in the gallery. Family ticket to admit 6 to the 2/- seats, 10/-and 6 to the 1/- seats, 5/-.

There was some light relief by the minstrels and the impressionist although the political, conservative elements in the programme are predictable – plenty of Empire plugging, with the dioramas of the Afghan and Zulu Wars. Victorian families in Preston witnessing these images of far-off lands with the latest technology – a miniature three-dimensional scene in which models of figures are seen against a background – would hardly have suspected that history would repeat itself with another war in Afghanistan by the time of the twenty-first century.

By contrast the good old standby of the Christmas pantomime season was offered on the 10 January 1880. It was marketed as Mr John Hudspeth's grand Christmas pantomime *Hop O' My Thumb*. For this performance the social needs of the poor were being considered with, 'Morning matinées on Saturday, half price for children of schools connected with the workhouse.' But there was little evidence of conciliation a year later in January 1881 for a performance of the pantomime *Babes in the Wood*, when the audience was described by *The Era* as those 'whose patronage bestowed is of the most wretched kind.' Reflecting on the progressing taste, there are dangers in stereotyping what may be perceived as a disorderly working-class audience.

The Theatre Royal offered family tickets in the 1880s, with other prices ranging from 6d to £1, implying bestowed respectability on family audiences who flocked to see the latest productions. Gone were the days of the theatre being regarded as an institution of dubious morality referred to by Whittle, with marathon programmes of three to four hours duration. The appeal of pantomime to Preston families would go some way to easing class divisions, for every provincial town had its own sparkle of the Christmas pantomime and this was mirrored in Preston.

'Mirror, mirror on the wall who is the fairest of them all?' In 1882 it was to be a new lessee and respected manager, Mr T. Ramsey, who improved and embellished the theatre to celebrate Preston Guild in 1882. A grand reopening night, with different performances each night of the Guild, consisted of military bands and three companies presenting opera and dramatic performances. The Guild Merchant festivities continued with a week of opera presented by the Royal English Opera Company commencing on the 11 September 1882. Adopting the nomenclature of the music hall, 'the management beg to announce that notwithstanding the enormous expense of the above Great Opera Company, including as it does the most eminent artists on the operatic stage; there will be no advance in the prices.' The performance on Thursday 14 September 1882 even featured the former manager of the theatre, William Parkinson, on the other side of the footlights, performing Manrico in Verdi's *Il Trovatore*.

The Theatre Royal was attracting more of a cross-class audience during the second half of the Victorian era. Most of the original tavern music halls closed during the 1880s, by which time the working classes were again being attracted to changing entertainment styles and the melodramas being staged at the theatre. Oscar Wilde visited the Preston theatre during 1884. 'The well-known aesthete is coming to Preston on the 13th instance to deliver a lecture on his personal impression of America. It maybe of interest to know, that Mr. Oscar Wilde is a nephew of the Revd Wilde, formerly of Whittle church, Chorley,' said *The Preston Chronicle*.

In 1898, the Theatre Royal underwent another renovation, which included adding three upper tiers giving a total capacity for 1,700: stalls, 100; boxes, 300; pit, 600; gallery, 700. The stage measured a depth of 40ft and a width of 50ft – height to fly rail, 20ft 6in, to grid, 42ft 6in, and 27ft to the proscenium arch. It reopened on the 9 November 1898 with corresponding reporting by the *Preston Guardian*: 'On Monday evening the Theatre Royal was opened to the public after having been entirely rebuilt. The new building is a very commodious one including the most modern improvements as to plan of construction, whilst the decorations are superbly handsome.' This development suggests that at the end of the nineteenth century the legitimate theatre was once again a dominant force in live entertainment in Preston, as it had adapted sufficiently to attract audiences from across the classes.

The rebuilt and extended theatre would have partly filled the void for the provision of live entertainment at a time when music hall was practically nonexistent elsewhere in Preston. Ongoing changes to the style of entertainment reflected its own brand of culture and featured Shakespeare, melodrama, revue, opera, and dramatic productions with touring actor-managers by the end of the nineteenth century. The local community could partake on stage with the first amateur operatic and dramatic societies. Gilbert and Sullivan's *Iolanthe* was staged by Preston Amateur Operatic Society on the 17 May 1889; during the same year, aspiring thespians could partake in a production of *Catherine Howard*, presented by Preston Amateur Dramatic Society on the 13 July 1889.

Gone But Not Forgotten
The twentieth century saw contemporary professional drama represented with Mr Edward Terry's London Theatre Company presenting five different plays at the Theatre Royal on the 10 December 1900. These included *Ben My Chree* and the religious melodrama *The Sign of the Cross* direct from the Prince's Theatre, London. The provincial theatre became a mirror of the London theatre and the standard achieved by the touring company must generally have outdone that of the original stock companies.

Nevertheless, the writing was on the wall for live entertainment and the theatre eventually succumbed to the competition of Edwardian music hall and a blossoming twentieth-century cinema. By 1911, Hugh Rain (Will Onda), the Preston cinema impresario, began showing the

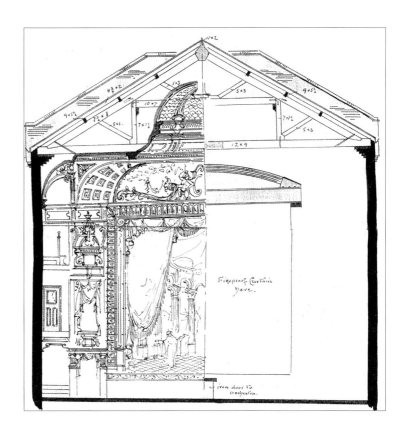

Right and below:
Original plans of the
Theatre Royal dated
1898. (Courtesy of
Lancashire Record
Office, PSPR2/224)

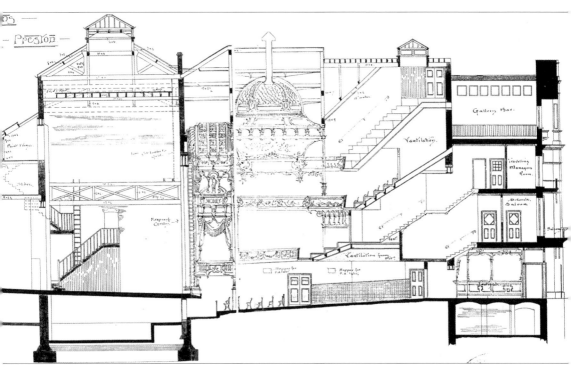

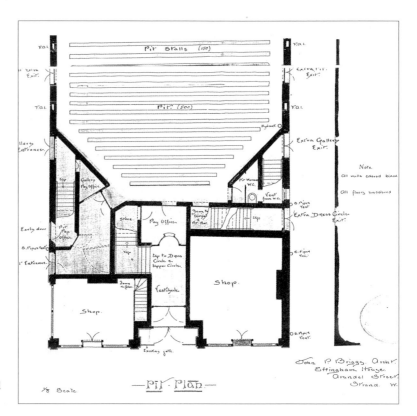

Plan of the Theatre Royal entrance and Pit Stalls.

latest revolution in entertainment at the time: silent films, a novel and new way of performing all the tricks expected of spectacular live melodrama. In May 1916, Mary Pickford starred in *Esmerelda* and 'Miss Amy Sissons of the Beecham Opera Company, Covent Garden, who vocally accompanies the pictures in perfect synchronisation, will appear at each performance.'

In November 1928 the theatre was adapted for sound pictures and no entertainers ever graced the stage again except on the silver screen. The *Lancashire Daily Post* reported as follows:

> Yesterday the Theatre Royal, Preston, the most historic place of amusement in the town, and until recently a small cosy building, was re-opened after undergoing re-construction and enlargement, a physical transformation, with the adaptation to the new and comprehensive ideas governing up-to-date cinema houses. The auditorium has been considerably extended both upstairs and down and, together with the new foyer, waiting rooms and entrance hall, has been lavishly decorated and upholstered. The orchestra and huge Christie Unit organ, which rise and sink at will from a sunken pit to stage level, provide music according to the modern scheme under the direction of Mr Harry Sainsbury, a musician who has had much distinguished service in Blackpool and London. The Theatre Royal has started on its latest phase of history.

During the 1950s I witnessed part of that history when seated high up in the gods of the Theatre Royal Cinema: I began to realise that the seats were very steeply banked and that the only way to see the screen properly was to look between the knees! While watching the film *The Dam Busters* my experience of this unusual position was to be a constant reminder to remain calm, because I felt that any slight disturbance might result in taking the shortest route to the stalls. Being one

The Theatre Royal in its adopted cinema role during the early 1950s. (Courtesy of Harris Reference Library, Preston)

step from heaven I discovered one reason why the top shelf was colloquially known as the gods, without consideration of the official explanation that it sprung from Greek mythology!

Sadly, June 1956 was the final curtain call for this grand old Preston building, where one thespian once announced from the stage that, 'the Preston theatre was the cosiest and best theatre in the whole of the provinces.' Nevertheless, it was reduced to a pile of rubble and replaced by the ultra-modern ABC Cinema. The new cinema was opened by Richard Todd on the 14 March 1959 and captured by Pathé news, who called it 'the most modern cinema of its day.' But such a momentous beginning could not prevent the closure of the cinema during 1982, after only twenty-three years. Change upon change is the story of Preston's entertainment industry and the site is now occupied by a modern retail store, albeit with a different type of dressing room. Theatre Street is an aptly named legacy and the only reminder today that a theatrical gem once stood proud serving the Victorians with their brand of popular culture throughout the whole of the so-called 'good old days'.

Voice from the Gods

'Stage Manager: please open the tabs to centre stage and instruct the maestro to give us a fanfare. Our venerable and charismatic chairman wishes to make an important announcement concerning legitimacy in the theatre.'

'Ladies and gentlemen: we now present an overview of the important legislation governing theatres and music hall to clarify the respective parameters, especially with regard to repertoire and good conduct.'

Left: The new ABC Cinema at the time of its opening in 1959. (Courtesy of *Lancashire Evening Post*)

Below: The site of the Theatre Royal as it is today. (M. Lockwood)

Intermission: Legitimate or Illegitimate Theatre?

On his return to the throne in 1660, Charles II made radical changes to the British theatre with the licensing of legitimate drama. The King issued patents restricting the right to run a theatre: these patents gave rights to build playhouses and to stage legitimate drama to only two London theatres, Covent Garden and the Theatre Royal. In 1737 the Lord Chamberlain took over the licensing of legitimate drama theatres and the patent theatres enjoyed a royal monopoly over spoken drama, although this monopoly came to be increasingly undermined: the Public General Act of 1788 gave magistrates the power to licence theatrical representations of plays that had been presented at the patent theatres for a period of sixty days.

The legal distinction between legitimate and illegitimate theatre was effectively abolished by Section One of the Theatres Act, 1843, which invoked theatre regulation throughout the country for a growing entertainment industry. The Theatres Act removed the traditional, or legitimate, theatre's monopoly so anyone could apply for a licence and present anything except drama in licensed premises. Owners could apply for a Lord Chamberlain's Licence, which authorised plays, or operate with a Liquor Licence issued by magistrates under the provision of the Disorderly Houses Act, 1751, which linked the sale of alcohol in pubs and taverns with the development of live music-hall entertainment. Music halls licensed by the local authority for music and dancing only were not allowed to stage plays or sketches. The Preston Theatre Royal was distinguished from music halls, which were denied the privilege of staging drama but allowed the running, sale and consumption of drink and tobacco in the auditorium. Conversely, the Theatre Royal could not be funded through alcohol served in the actual auditorium.

In June 1904 the following statement (abridged) was published by the Theatrical Manager's Association:

> Theatres have been for the last sixty years regulated under the Stage Plays Act of 1843. The Act provides for the licensing of theatres and the censorship by the Lord Chamberlain of all performances taking place therein. Music halls are licensed under an older act, which does not impose any censorship or restriction upon the performances to be given; but at the same time it does not in any way sanction the performance of stage plays. In the course of time there has arisen a practice of presenting at music halls, in addition to variety entertainment consisting of songs, dance and other performances, slight sketches with two or three performers and lasting about quarter of an hour. Agreement concerning the issue of sketches and dramatic performances in music hall was reached in 1912 and the music halls then came under the jurisdiction of the Lord Chamberlain. This dramatically increased the scope of entertainment offered at the nation's theatres and was mirrored at Preston.

From 1737-1968 all theatrical performances and stage plays needed the approval of the Lord Chamberlain's Office and scripts had to be submitted before a licence was issued authorising the performance. The Theatres Act, 1968, effectively lifted the jurisdiction of the Lord Chamberlain and abolished censorship. To this day theatres do not require music and dancing licences for incidental music to a play or for music or dancing forming part of a performance such as a musical comedy or ballet. Apart from this exception a theatre licence does not cover public music or dancing.

The Effect of the Theatres Act, 1843 in Preston

The first singing saloons and concert halls were licensed under the liberally interpreted Disorderly Houses Act, 1751, and the economy of the halls was governed by the sale and consumption of the intoxicating liquor that funded the entertainment. Breaches of the Theatres Act, 1843, were rare in Preston, but in the 1870s, with the introduction of sketches into music hall, there were grounds for complaint by rival theatre managers. The manager of the Theatre Royal identified rival illegal theatrical activity when he saw a contravention of the law at the George Concert Hall during September 1876, when the landlord was fined 10s and costs for allowing stage plays to be performed without a theatrical licence. In fact, it was a comic routine sketch with dialogue between two artists and lasting only a few minutes. The reaction of the Theatre Royal's manager indicates a keen sense of rivalry with music hall and a protection of his repertoire in what was a competitive commercial environment.

The Theatre Royal gradually introduced elements of music-hall and circus entertainment. However, one stipulation of the legislation precluded drinking and smoking in the auditorium, but this too appears to have been rarely contravened. An example is Edward Gibbons who, in 1868, was charged with being drunk and smoking in the theatre. 'He was locked away because of the many complaints,' according to Edward Tannent, the stage manager. He 'cautioned all persons against smoking as the respectable portion of the audience had been obliged to leave the audience the previous evening. At the subsequent court appearance, the mayor, acting as magistrate, wished it to be understood that smoking was against the regulations and fined him 1s or seven days in jail.' The above are two examples of the 1843 Act being applied in Preston but what do they imply about the development of music hall?

The Gibbons case not only illustrates the working of the Theatres Act (1843), but also shows how music hall was initially perceived as lacking the respectability of middle-class entertainment. The Act can thus be said to have helped to formalise music hall as, primarily, a working-class form of entertainment where workers found some escape from their hard lives in the factories in an atmosphere of enhanced conviviality. This example of the 1843 Act being applied in Preston illustrates the attraction of music hall for a significant number of customers, like Gibbons, who were able to smoke, drink, enjoy the entertainment and savour the working-class, bawdy atmosphere of the pub music hall without finding themselves on the wrong side of the law. For many, a lively and varied evening would have been preferable to an uncomfortable seat in the gallery at the legitimate theatre at a cost of around 3d.

The 1843 Act thus demarcates music hall as a genre and formalises its economic link with alcohol. Theatre proprietors could not fund their performances through alcohol in the auditorium and had to rely on seat prices alone. From its inception in Preston, as elsewhere, music hall grew from and appealed to a working-class culture where workers formulated their own distinct form of entertainment in the pubs in contrast to the programmes on offer at the purpose-built theatre. In the music hall the working-class audience was central rather than peripheral. However, during the second half of the nineteenth century the contest between theatre and music hall was not as one-sided as may first appear due to the increasing appeal of pantomime, seasonal music hall, revue, melodrama, and Shakespeare to all classes of society, both in Preston and in other English towns and cities.

In 1945, a local man, Harry Pye, recalled visiting the Theatre Royal during the Victorian era and his account illustrated a need for increased legislation governing good conduct and safety procedures in theatres. 'Then there were the plays and pantomimes at the Theatre Royal. I remember the uncontrolled crush at the pit and gallery doors, in the days before the queue-system had been invented.' Harry witnessed events that were not without precedent and the quotation highlights the effect of the theatre's own brand of culture on audiences and the popularity of the pit and gallery with audiences, some of whom had to be of a certain energetic constitution to survive even getting into the theatre.

We will see how safety and reformative considerations led to the legislative process taking a different cue which led to a reduction of theatrical and music-hall provision in Preston and indeed throughout England during the late Victorian era.

Scene Three: 'From a Gin Palace to a King's Palace'

The first music-hall proprietors capitalised on a potentially lucrative market with a gradual adoption of acts derived from the incorporation of elements from a plethora of earlier forms of entertainment. Preston parallels similar events throughout England with a phased development of Victorian music hall. Music Hall gradually evolved from the first singing saloons of the 1840s and '50s into the more elaborate and commercialised George Music Hall of 1864 and the King's Palace of 1913, but crucial to the development of the drink and music-hall industry in Preston was the influence of temperance. It follows that the temperance movement was especially active in Preston, campaigning against drunkenness and low moral standards the city's growing number of public houses and singing saloons throughout much of the Victorian era.

The spirit duty was reduced throughout England in 1825 and the revenue from spirits rose, with a consequential rise in the number of retail spirit outlets. The scale of drunkenness was therefore at first directed towards the consumption of spirits rather than beer. Ironically, attempts to liberate the era of the gin palaces came with the succession of the beer trade and corresponding legislation which provided that, on payment of a £2 licence fee, anyone could set up a house selling beer only. Not surprisingly, the Beer Shop Act of 1830 exacerbated the local drink problem when it brought around 190 beerhouses to Preston between 1830 and 1834, and therefore the implementation of this legislation is likely to have fuelled the temperance cause with which the movement coincided.

Beer shops or houses were judged to be a haven for thieves and prostitutes and their overall tone stimulated newspaper correspondents and reformers to vigorously attack the subculture in the liberal press:

> In another beer-house, fiddling and singing is the order of the night; in every one it is vice with the paint off, for most, if not all, of the men, are thieves or worse, and the women, without exception, are prostitutes of the lowest and most depraved class. Here they are unmistakeably plying their horrid vocation, drinking almost fiercely. Cards and dominoes appear to be great favourites, but it does not appear that they are gambling, perhaps because they have nothing to gamble for.

Despite the colourful language, entertainment in pubs and beerhouses is evident during 1838, when 'boys and girls aged between fourteen and seventeen years, without a guardian present, played pitch and toss and danced to a fiddle overnight in a jerry shop (beerhouse)'. This sort of activity during the 1830s can be seen as the beginning of the genre of 'free and easies'. The level of poverty and vice affecting young people in the first 'free and easies' in beerhouses is encapsulated in the following account, written in 1865, coinciding with the end of the Cotton Famine: 'In one low dirty room of a beerhouse crowded with young men and low prostitutes, a fiddler is scraping away at an old fiddle and a girl is step dancing.'

The girl's step dancing represents a link with a local tradition in the cotton mills where a large workforce of women would start beating out a rhythm with their wooden clogs in time to the shuttles buzzing back and forth on the loom. Step-dancing or 'Lancashire Clog', became

THE ENGLISH JUGGERNAUT.

'The Struggle'. The Temperance movement was synonymous with opposition to the development of Victorian music hall and the drinks industry.

a favourite with mill-workers in Preston. Clog dancing was performed extensively in music hall, representing a strong northern culture and perhaps even solidarity and local pride during Preston's Industrial Revolution.

The description 'free and easy' could apply to many premises throughout the nineteenth century, where workers sang to musical accompaniment in pubs and beerhouses and where informality stimulated entertainment. A report in 1868 on a 'free and easy' at the Old Cock Inn noted there were '40 gentlemen present, with excellent singing and a brass and string band.' The usual practice was that customers would sing popular songs with perhaps the landlord playing the piano, exemplified at the Park Road Inn in February 1870: 'George Marginson will open on Saturday evening, a free and easy, for adults only. A competent pianist will be in attendance and no expense will be spared to render it attractive and respectable.'

The impromptu tavern 'free and easy' entertainment was distinct from entertainment in purpose-built concert halls, increasingly known as music halls by the mid-nineteenth century. The phrase 'music hall' was probably first used as a euphemism for miscellaneous entertainment. In the early years of the genre, the two names 'music hall', and 'variety' were used interchangeably. The New Surrey Music Hall (*c.* 1840), and the Music Hall, Hungerford Market, are early instances of the names given to music halls in the area of London. The phrase 'theatre of varieties,' appeared as early as 1829 with the name 'Regency Theatre of Varieties,' Tottenham Street, London. However, overall theories suggest that the late Victorian term for a variety theatre was 'music hall', also known as concert halls/rooms or singing saloons.

In London, Charles Morton traditionally pioneered music hall in December 1849. Morton gave concert performances on three nights a week at the Canterbury Arms, Lambeth. In 1852, Morton opened an adjacent concert hall, significantly separate from the public house. Charles Morton presented ballet and opera in concert form as well as variety and is known to have presented the first performance of Gounod's *Faust*, sung in English. Morton was known as 'the father of the halls', but can he lay claim to the very first purpose-built music hall?

Although historians search for the identity of the very first English music hall, its identity is a bit like the search for the Holy Grail. Was it, for example, the 1829 Regency Theatre of Varieties, Tottenham Street, London? Thomas Sharples opened the Bolton Star Music Hall in 1832, which is generally accepted as one of the earliest in England.

Though not as early as the Bolton Star, the establishment of a purpose-built concert room or music hall first came to Preston with the opening of the Albion in 1839, which places Preston at the forefront of national music-hall growth, with a concert room cable of accommodating up to 600 people. Prison chaplain the Revd John Clay provides evidence of three extant early Preston concert halls in his 1842 Annual Report: 'One of the concert rooms, capable of holding 650 persons was opened in the summer of 1839. Two others of smaller dimension were opened in the spring of 1841.' Therefore a pattern of growth and evidence of the commercialisation and regularity of the industry begins to emerge.

During December 1841, the *Chronicle* advertised the Albion public house, Clarke's Yard, Preston, for rent with two sizeable concert rooms: 'To be let the 'Albion' with well accustomed spirit vault and two concert rooms measuring 52' x 29' and 55' x 31' and with tap rooms attached thereto.' The continuity of the Albion is supported by the 1851 Census Enumerator's Report which, for the first time, describes occupants as five professional vocalists: three men and one woman in their twenties, and one nineteen-year-old male musician. The presence of professional artists and the very fact that the Albion had such large separate concert rooms provides evidence that the Albion was the first established music hall in Preston.

At the time of the Theatres Act of 1843, the market for commercial entertainment was already being exploited by publicans in pubs and beerhouses with the gradual adoption of music-hall acts derived from diverse sources. Liberal consumption of alcohol was a driving economic force behind the growing popularity of live entertainment with capital investment being made by some landlords in adapting their public houses and beerhouses to accommodate live entertainment.

On a visit to Preston in 1851 James Hudson commented: 'singing rooms are numerous, prosperous and constantly well attended.' There were numerous unrefined and modified singing saloons in public houses and beerhouses throughout the town incorporating live amateur and some professional engagements. In 1852 there were said to be 'public houses in every part of Preston and its vicinity and nearly in every nook and corner.'[31] This is not just an indication of the number of places serving alcohol, some of which were embryonic music halls, but shows that workers had money they were ready to spend in the pubs and on entertainment. Indeed, by 1868 the combined total of beerhouses and public houses had reached approximately 490 premises throughout the town.

During January 1865, the *Chronicle* reported on the Black Swan Concert Hall situated on Water Street, Preston. Here, the basic accommodation consisted of a 'concert hall measuring 20' x 16', cheap decorations, a little stage and rough wooden seats occupied by sixty or seventy lads and lassies of the cotton-operative class. Young girls gaudily dressed were seated supping porter which they had exchanged for a refreshment ticket.' Early music hall was governed by the sale and consumption of the intoxicating liquor that funded the entertainment.

The concert rooms operated a token system for admission, known as a refreshment ticket or 'wet money', exchanged for alcohol at the bar. The Revd John Clay described the basic economics of music hall at this stage of its evolution. 'The man or woman pays two-pence to entitle them to admission, for which they receive a ticket, and for that ticket they receive two pennyworth of liquor, and the dramatic representation.' In Preston a link between music hall and public house expansion can be seen in the prospering pub trade of the 1860s and '70s, which may be linked to increases in workers' earnings and increased leisure time. The music-hall boom of the 1860s was at its peak at a time when beer and gin in the pubs were inexpensive and the economics of the music hall hinged on the sale of alcohol. At the very moment the economy began to recover from the effects of the Cotton Famine, some landlords adapted public houses and beerhouses so as to provide for live public entertainment. The opening of the George Music Hall in November 1864, when 'hundreds were refused admission to prevent suffocation,' illustrates how successfully they timed their strategy.

Migration from rural areas to the urban environment of Preston was extensive for those seeking employment. For example, at the time of the 1861 census, Edward Blackoe was a thirty-two-year-old farrier born at Haighton, near Preston but then living with his brother John in Friargate, Preston. The entrepreneurial Blackoe brothers moved from the nearby hamlet to exploit the pub and music-hall industry and showed business acumen in the part they played in the emerging music-hall industry by opening two purpose-built concert halls, both situated in Friargate, thereby providing the real foundation for music hall in Preston. Edward Blackoe

Refreshment token for the George Inn whilst under the proprietorship of Leo Waddington. The inscription reads, 'Waddington's Concert Hall', George Inn, Preston. (Courtesy of P. Vickers)

Wilton's Music Hall in London's East End.

Site of the George Music Hall, Friargate, as it is today.

opened the 'George Concert Room', on Saturday 29 November 1864 and John Blackoe opened the New King's Head Concert Hall, Preston on the 14 November 1870, though by 1869 the Trade Directory shows a Leo Waddington as proprietor of the George Inn.

The George was an ambitious purpose-built hall constructed at the rear of the pub as a separate adjunct with audience capacity for 1,000. It measured 93ft long by 24ft wide and was 16ft high with an arched roof, properly ventilated, with good seats and a stage with beautiful scenery. This building draws a parallel with Wilton's Music Hall, built in 1858 in London's East End and believed to be the oldest surviving example of an early concert hall and which broadly corresponds with the description of the George.

The Preston Chronicle advertised the opening of the George:

> Edward Blackoe of the 'George Inn', Friargate, intends to open, a new and very extensive concert room, built expressly for the purpose… First class talent has been engaged and nothing will be wanted to make entertainment pleasing, happy and comfortable, so that even the most fastidious may go and spend a few jovial hours to their heart's content.

Over 1,000 patrons attended the opening night and Blackoe announced, 'this is living proof that the people of Preston will support entertainments when they are of a good and respectable character. The hall will be opened every evening about seven o'clock and closed about ten.'

At the George:

> There was nothing calculated to disgust or demoralise… The curtain rose and the usual concert-hall swell, dressed in loud and utterly impossible attire, came upon the stage. Upon the stage, in one corner sat a rubicund-looking chairman who announced the coming man… after a well-merited encore the curtain fell and the orchestra played selections until the chairman announced another singer.

The presence of a chairman and formalised programming is further evidence of a greater level of organisation underpinned by good management.

John Blackoe was obviously convinced of the demand for popular entertainment, as he followed his brother's lead in claiming the King's Head as the largest and most respectable concert hall in town by the time of its 1870 opening. The opening of purpose-built concert halls is consistent with the pace of the industry and national music-hall development. Preston was compact in area, mainly because of the working-class housing density; any reasonably fit adult could walk anywhere in the town in under half an hour to reach the legitimate theatre or concert hall.

The inclusive seating capacity in eight of Preston's concert halls, plus seasonal music-hall productions at the Theatre Royal, gives an estimated capacity of between 7,000-8,000 seats for music hall during the Victorian apogee of the late 1860s and early 1870s. This served a steadily rising population that had increased by 3.5 per cent to 85,427 by the time of the 1871 census. According to Bailey (1986):'After the take off in the 1850s music hall enjoyed its first great boom in the 1860s and early 1870s.' Preston broadly corresponds with the national expansion of the Victorian music-hall industry, though there are difficulties in quantifying the exact number of concert halls/music halls as there was often no differentiation between a pub offering free and easy entertainment and a purpose-built hall. The Preston boom was further evidenced with the opening of the 'Guild Music Hall' in October 1866 when 'long before the performance commenced the room was full to repletion,' but it was nevertheless advertised for lease by February 1867.

A GRAND NEW CONCERT HALL FOR PRESTON.

JOHN BLAKOE,

KING'S HEAD INN FRIARGATE,

Begs to inform the public of Preston and neighbourhood, that he intends to Open on Monday the 14th of November (nightly) a

NEW CONCERT HALL,

which will be the largest and most respectable in the town. First Class Talent have already been engaged, and nothing will be wanted to make the Entertainments worthy the appreciation of a really respectbble audience.

Good Ale, Good Spirits, Good Order.

Good Music, Good Talent; and Respectable treatment always on hand.

Remember Monday, November the 14th is the date fixed for the opening.

Opening of the King's Head Concert Hall, Friargate, as advertised in *The Preston Chronicle*, 5 November 1870.

KING'S HEAD NEW CONCERT HALL, FRIARGATE, PRESTON.
Sole Proprietor, Mr. JOHN BLACKOE.

ANOTHER GRAND CHANGE.

On MONDAY, February 6th, and during the week, the following talented artistes will appear :—

Messrs. WRIGHT and SADLER, Great Duettists. Miss LIZZIE GLENVILLE, the Fascinating Serio Comic. Miss FLORENCE WASHINGTON, the great American Clog, Pump, Boot, and Skate Dancer. JERRY FARRISEY, Irish Comedian and Dancer.

This place of amusement is now fitted up with Atkinson's Patent Heating Apparatus, and is acknowledged to be the most comfortable Hall in Preston.

Leader, Mr. H. F. COLLIER; pianist, Mr. T. MC.ARDLE; cornet, Mr. S. COLLINSON; GEO. D'ARCY, Manager.

N.B.—Select room, with private entrance, commanding a full view of the Stage.

P.S.—The Harmonic Room is open every Evening at 10 o'clock.

A diverse programme at the King's Head Concert Hall for February 1871; note that the Harmonic Room is open every evening at 10 p.m.

Albion Hotel, Church Street	1839 – c. 1856
Wagon and Horses, Tithebarn Street	c. 1859 – c. 1868
Crown Music Hall, Church Street	1872 – 1874
George Hotel, Friargate	1864 – 1889
Black Swan, Water Street	c. 1865 – 1880s
Guild Inn, Library Street	1866 – 1870
Sun Inn, Main Sprit Weind	1870 – 1874
New King's Head, Friargate	1870 – 1882

Victorian music hall featured clog dancers and novelty acts, musicians, jugglers, ventriloquists, clowns and circus-inspired acts. Comedy, in a variety of styles, was a vital part of Preston's evolutionary music-hall repertoire, with serio-comics featuring prominently. Another key figure to emerge in Preston music hall was the singer, whether he was a comic, duettist, sentimental ballad or operatic singer. While popular songs could help draw the working-class audience there is some evidence of a broad musical culture in music hall, especially so at Sun Inn, with an operatic vocalist appearing in 1870.

The diversity of performance styles at these halls began to appeal to a wider audience. The level of sophistication was sometimes wanting, especially when Miss McDonald appeared at the Crown Inn Music Hall, Church Street in October 1863. The *Chronicle* advertised as her as 'Miss McDonald the Scottish giantess – the largest woman in the three kingdoms who may be seen for a short time at the Crown Inn, Church Street.' This type of performance alludes to the travelling fairground booths that visited Preston, but wow, she must have been quite a size!

By contrast, an attempt to sound a cultured tone was expressed at the George in September 1872, when landlord Mr Leo Waddington advertised 'the last week of Don Ferretra – playing the flute at the George. All should come and see this clever artist before his departure from England.'

THE GUILD CONCERT HALL AT PRESTON TO LET.—TO BE LET, the Guild Concert-Hall, with the refreshment-rooms attached, situate in Library-street, Preston. The Concert-room, which is capable of accomodating upwards of 600 persons, is beautifully and appropriately decorated, and is nightly visited by a very numerous and respectable audience. Attached to the premises is an excellent BEERHOUSE, fitted with first-class brewing plant, which may be taken along with the Concert Hall, or separately. — Apply to Mr. HENRY ASPDEN (the lessee) on the premises. None but respectable and experienced parties need to offer.

Preston Chronicle advert from 1867 concerning the lease of the Guild Music Hall.

SECOND-HAND PIANOFORTES,
NEARLY NEW.

THESE INSTRUMENTS have only been used during the present Season, and will be sold cheap. All are warranted.

PIANOFORTES, HARMONIUMS, and every description of MUSICAL INSTRUMENT TUNED and REPAIRED by first-class workmen.

THE LATEST MUSIC at HALF-PRICE.

PARCEL FROM LONDON DAILY.

J. NORWOOD,
PIANOFORTE AND HARMONIUM ROOMS,
91, FISHERGATE, PRESTON.

DANCING.—Mr. BRUSSELL'S Derby Assembly-room, Stoneygate. Public Assembly every Saturday, Monday, and Wednesday nights, at 7·80. Brussell's full band in attendance. Tuesday nights for learners only. Juveniles at Seven; 3d. each. Adults at Eight; 6d. each. Private parties can be accommodated by band and rooms on Thursday or Friday nights on very reasonable terms. A Juvenile Class from Three to Five o'clock on Saturdays; 8d. each.

SUN INN MUSIC HALL
MAIN SPIRIT WEIND.
PROPRIETOR:—Mr. JOSEPH EDWARDS, Late of Farington.

J. E. begs to announce to his friends and the public of Preston, that he has ENTERED on the ABOVE ESTABLISHMENT, and hopes by strict attention to business to merit a share of public patronage.

HARMONIC ROOM open every evening at Seven o'clock.—Pianist:—J. WOODS.

CUNARD
ROYAL MAIL STEAMERS.
FROM LIVERPOOL
DIRECT TO NEW YORK AND BOSTON.

PARTHIA.	CALABRIA.	TARIFA.
SCOTIA.	BATAVIA.	ABYSSINIA.
CUBA.	SIBERIA.	JAVA.
SAMARIA.	ALGERIA.	HECLA.
ALEPPO.	RUSSIA.	MALTA.
PALMYRA.	CHINA.	TRIPOLI.

The CUNARD ROYAL MAIL STEAMERS sail every TUESDAY THURSDAY, and SATURDAY, and have superior accommodation for Cabin and Steerage passengers.

Passengers can purchase their Tickets from the Cunard Agents as low a price as they can obtain them in Liverpool.

Contemporary adverts in a newspaper column of 1872 featuring the Sun Inn. By now Victorians could emigrate to North America or stay at home and indulge in home entertainment with the pianoforte.

Performance Styles in the Victorian Music Halls of Preston (compiled by the author)

Venue and Date	Programme	Remarks
Guild Concert Hall, Library Street, Rear of St John's church. *Preston Chronicle*, 6.10.1866.	Messrs Snape, Culliver and Robson, Negro Comedians; Will Vale, comique; Miss Julia Smythe, sentimental and serio-comic.	Serio-comics dominate.
Theatre Royal Music Hall, Fishergate. *Preston Chronicle*, 16.3.1867	Monsieur Caselli, first appearance out of London of the wonder of the world. Performing and juggling on the invisible wire; Master Shapcott, vocalist, dancer and drummer.	Circus and music hall.
The Sun, Main Sprit Weind. *The Era*, 11.9.1870	Madam Lorenzo (sentimental and operatic vocalist), a talented artist; Nelly Gilton (serio-comic – also very clever); Signor Saroni (piccolo player and baritone vocalist who is constantly demanded).	Evidence of refined culture.
King's Head. *The Era*, 28.1.72	'Professor Capron – ventriloquist; F. Raymond – impersonator and clog dancer; The Brothers Panell – French clowns with performing dogs; Miss Amy Turner and Miss B. Anderson – serio comic; Miss Jessie Danvers – vocalist and clog dancer; Tom Melbourne – star comic.	Clog dancers typical music-hall fare in Preston.
George Concert Hall, Friargate. *The Era*, 21.7.1878	Tom and Rose Merry (duettists, vocalists and dancers); Marie Santley (serio-comic); Will Atkins (comic); Mr and Mrs Patrick Miles and Young Ireland (known as the solid man) and Tom Walker, described as topical.	Presented generic music-hall acts 1864–1889.

As the music-hall industry took off success led to alterations in practically every hall. Martin Brown took over the George in 1874. As an established music-hall comedian who had entertained at the King's Head, Preston in December 1870, Martin would have had knowledge of the business in his new role at the George. New ideas included an extension for continuous twelve-hour music-hall performances at the George on Whit Monday 1876. *The Era* advertised: 'Uninterrupted performances on Whit Monday (only) from 10 a.m. to 10 p.m. with the concert room being crowded most of the time.' This mirrors a continuing demand for music hall with a large cast incorporating traditional music-hall acts.

The economics of the business were such that the George Music Hall had to be maintained to a high standard with improved theatrical facilities and additional dressing rooms. Accordingly, following a short period of closure for refurbishment, the reopening was subsequently reported in the October 1879 edition of *The Era*:

It was reopened on Monday last and was literally packed with a most respectable audience with crowds being unable to gain admission. The hall has undergone extensive alterations with the stage remodelled, new commodities and dressing rooms provided, fresh scenery supplied and the place decorated tastefully. With a good band occupying the orchestra place, it promises one of the first attractions of the town.

But not for much longer; the building of the Harris Museum and Art Gallery led to the closure and the eventual demolition of the original George Public House and Music Hall in 1895. The George had functioned as a music hall in its own right for twenty-five years and as such was a clear precursor to the New Gaiety Palace of Varieties, Tithebarn Street, which opened in 1882.

The Gaiety, like so many music halls, had its origins in performing impresarios who exploited the market by opening permanent theatres on the site of earlier constructions during the mid-nineteenth century. For example, Blackpool's Grand Theatre, though never a regular music hall, was built on the site of OHMY's old wooden pavilion circus building in 1884. To exploit the growing number of visitors to Preston, a wooden construction occupied by Newsome's Circus was constructed east of the railway station in Butler Street in 1872. The convenient railway station location capitalised on the circus attraction for passengers on local excursions and special trains:

> Newsome's Grand Circus – adjoining the railway station, Butler Street, Preston. Immense success of last night's *Cinderella* – notice to the inhabitants of Longridge, Goosnargh, Fulwood and neighbourhood, a special train will leave Preston tomorrow, Thursday evening at a quarter to eleven, for the accommodation of parties from that locality visiting the circus.

Famous names of the circus ring visited Preston including the clown 'Professor Storelli', who was billed as 'the funniest fiddler in the world' when he performed at Newsome's Circus at Preston in June 1880. Prices were relatively high at 3s, 2s, 1s, 6d.

Newsome remained at this site until October 1880, when the original building was adapted by Henry Hemfrey, a local comedian and impresario, who transformed Newsome's wooden circus pavilion for theatrical use and named it 'The Gaiety Temperance Theatre of Varieties.' *The Era* documented the proceedings and style of performance:

> The wooden structure recently vacated by Mr Newsome has been fitted up as a theatre and is at present occupied by a concert hall party under the guidance of Mr H. Hemfrey. A large audience has assembled. The building has undergone a wonderful metamorphism and for comfort, elegance and convenience could not be improved. The artists at present engaged are: Mr Tom Callaghan, comic and dancer; Mon Descombes – globe performer and juggler; Madam Laura invisible wire equilibrist; Miss Julia Bullen – serio-comic; Sisters Coulson – duettists and dancers, acrobats and contortionists; Jolly Little Lewis, comic; Messrs Clifford and Franks… Admission prices: chairs 1/-, sides and promenade 6d, pit 3d, half price to chairs at nine.

By 1882 the original 'Gaiety Temperance Theatre' stood in the way of proposed railway station expansion into Butler Street and was demolished. Sole proprietor Henry Hemfrey transferred to the 'New Gaiety Palace of Varieties, situated in Tithebarn Street, complete with fixed pit and gallery seats and a properly equipped stage with capacity for 2,000 patrons in the large architecturally designed auditorium.' Thus was born Preston's first commodious purpose-built music-hall staging predominantly generic variety and circus entertainment and completely detached from licensed premises. The New Gaiety heralded competition on a much grander scale by eclipsing the original wooden pavilion and several singing saloons and was heir to Newsome's Circus of 1872 and the transformed Gaiety of 1880.

The opening of the New Gaiety coincided with the September Guild of 1882 and included midnight performances of the grand Guild Company. Traditional circus acts continued to feature in music hall hybridising both circus and music-hall acts. On the 7 July 1884, the Gaiety Palace of Varieties featured the Wondrous Panlos performing acrobatically whilst on roller skates; Little Ernest the Midget Clown; jugglers, acrobats, a marionette show, dancers, musicians, trick cyclists, Tyrolean Minstrels and Percy Honri – 'Champion Boy Tenor of the World'.

Preston mirrored the national trend of dispensing with the music-hall chairman presiding over the proceedings and it is likely that the acts were indicated by a board side-stage with a list of numbers in the programme giving the order of the artists' appearances. Admission to the best seats was 1s, pit 6d and gallery 3d. These admission prices were the same as those at the original Gaiety Temperance Theatre in Butler Street. The tradition of music hall being a working-class male preserve was beginning to change for there is some evidence that respectable families were being attracted to the Gaiety Music Hall during 1884 where, judging by the programme, a high level of discipline was apparent: 'Police in attendance and strict order enforced.' Female

THE NEW GAIETY
Palace of Varieties,
TITHEBARN STREET, PRESTON.
Sole Proprietor and Manager - - Mr. HARRY HEMFREY.

The Grand New Hall.

The most popular place of Amusement in Preston. Everybody should see this Magnificent Establishment. See the following

GUILD COMPANY:

THE SISTERS AND BROTHER PHILLIPS. MESSRS. VERN AND VOLT. MONS. TULA, SILLO, AND ZETTI. MIACO. HARRY DALE. HARRY CARSDALE. LOUIE. ELLIOTTE, and others.

Splendid Band. New Scenery, and the Best Entertainment in Preston.

Everyday Performances as follows:—

Morning at 11-30; Afternoon at 3; Evening at 7. Midnight Perform- ances on Monday, Thursday and Friday; doors open at 11 30; Overture at 12.

Prices of Admission: 1s., 6d., and 3d.

The New Gaiety Place of Varieties music-hall programme at the time of its opening, which coincided with the Preston Guild of 1882.

attendance was encouraged but prostitutes were discouraged by the inducement of 'Thursday nights: ladies free if accompanied by a gentleman but children must be paid for.'

By now refreshment tokens for alcohol had long since disappeared as a means of funding the performance. The original Gaiety Theatre, Butler Street, was given the full title of Gaiety Temperance Theatre when it opened on 18 October 1880. At the New Gaiety Palace of Varieties there was no theatre bar in 1882 and drinking patrons were directed to the Harmonic Room at the Wagon and Horses. Therefore, both the old and the new Gaiety Theatres illustrate the changing role of drink during the 1880s in the development of music-hall economics.

The temperance movement was in continual conflict with music hall through much of its development and its influence prevailed in Preston well into the twentieth century. William Henry Broadhead was himself an advocate of temperance and many of his theatres, including the Palace and the Hippodrome, never had liquor licences until after his death in 1930. Unlike the Victorian music hall, reliance on alcohol as a source of funding was evidently unimportant and the crush rooms and lounges of Broadhead's two Preston theatres offered only soft drinks and cups of tea. It was not until November in 1933 that plans for the King's Palace show new refreshment rooms incorporating two bars, each situated at the rear of the stalls and circle.

The opening of brand-new variety theatres during the last two decades of the nineteenth century represented the peak growth of British music hall. By the first decade of the twentieth century the music hall had mass appeal as impresarios and syndicate owners capitalised on the resurgent Edwardian demand for the culture of the music hall. The culmination of music-hall progression in Preston came with a battle for the King's Palace when rival theatre owners objected to the granting of the licence for its 1913 opening. Circuit owner William Henry Broadhead emerged as the victor for the Palace, proudly announcing: 'Another Messrs Broadhead & Sons achievement in the raising of magnificent halls for the delectation of the people. This is the most up to date theatre in Lancashire offering opera from the Grand Junction, Manchester and pantomime from the Pavilion, Liverpool.'

Overall it can be seen that Victorian music hall evolved from circus and other entertainment forms such as street ballad singers and from the free and easy entertainment in pubs and beerhouses transposing to singing rooms and concert rooms in public houses that in turn gave impetus to music-hall development and the introduction of theatrical conditions in variety theatres. The economic conditions prevailing in the first decade of the twentieth century were to provide a fertile ground for the establishment of the first Edwardian music hall in Preston and the town can be seen to be a suitable microcosm reflecting national, or, at least, London-based Victorian music-hall development.

Voice from the Gods

'To the inhabitants of Preston: Engaged at a great expense are stars of well-known celebrity who will appear in rapid succession. Before bringing up the tabs, the chairman wishes to announce that scene four will explore the audience's composition, thus determining why the Victorian music hall in Preston was a particular target for advocates of temperance and social reformers who attacked the subculture of the music-hall industry and successfully achieved a degree of reform. The venerable chairman also seeks clarification as to whether there was such a clear division between reformers and rational recreation on the one side and music-hall proprietors advocating respectability on the other. Judge for yourselves, for all will be revealed.'

Scene Four: 'Let's All Go to the Music Hall'

Audience Composition and Attacks on the Victorian Pub and Music-Hall Industry
Victorian Music hall and the legitimate theatre in Preston were both popular but there were clear distinctions of social class and segregation of audiences, usually relating to the cost of admission. Naturally, working-class people were economically minded during times of unemployment and music hall had a strong and widespread appeal in attracting those who perhaps wished to be distracted from the hardships of urban living during 'Hard Times,' not only by consuming inexpensive beer and gin but also by the conviviality of the music hall. Audience behaviour and segregation was determined by those who entered the theatre through a separate outside entrance to the gallery or pit, as distinctive from the persona of those in the dress circle and front stalls. Bratton (1986) records: 'A packed auditorium contained an audience that was not one group but many. The old division of box, pit and gallery fragmented into class, sex, money and age old social distinctions.'[30]

This ideology I perceive as drawing a parallel with the huge King's Palace Theatre, Preston. In its dying years and immediately prior to demolition I observed the separate street entrances with the faded words stalls, pit and gallery through which generations of the townsfolk, including my forebears, had passed. I pondered while reflecting that the battle for the once proud King's Palace had finally been lost though the story of music hall in Preston still had many a tale to tell.

Away from the rows of terraced slums of Victorian Preston there seems little doubt that young people of both sexes frequented the earliest music halls. Joseph Livesey testified in 1834 that he had no objection to either music or dancing in the beer shops and pubs of Preston, provided there was some official regulation. Social reformers saw this style of impromptu entertainment staged in the first free and easies as likely to expose young people to moral danger, and thus, in its earliest form, music hall was under attack on moral grounds.

Correspondents to *The Preston Chronicle* were already expressing doubts about the 'New Singing Rooms' as early as 1841:

> Sir, permit me through the medium of your paper to make some enquiries and observations concerning the singing rooms which have of late become established in various parts of town. I am informed that individuals from the age of 12 and upwards of 60 years of age are to be found attending these rooms. Intoxicating liquors are also sold on the spot.

Also during 1841 moral concerns were expressed over certain heinous events witnessed by another *Chronicle* correspondent in town-centre singing rooms. She wrote:

> I myself know an instance of the seduction of an unfortunate female, who had been enticed to attend a singing room, contrary to the orders of her mistress, and who lost her good name and her good place in consequence… I have known married men frequent singing rooms with the most infamous and disgraceful intentions. Now for the third grave charge against singing rooms: I have known lads of fourteen or fifteen years of age being encouraged to squander the money of their employers, which they had purloined, and to bring along with them girls of vile character, upon whom they spend considerable sums in liquor.

The concert room atmosphere of certain early forms of music hall suggests excessive consumption of alcohol, sexual impropriety and a level of criminal activity. It is interesting to note that the concerns expressed here are not simply for the welfare of members of the working-class, but for the interests of the middle–class also, as a mistress has lost her servant and employers are troubled by theft.

The King's Palace Theatre, Preston; performances at 6.40 and 9 p.m. (Drawing by C. Dodding)

The social concerns of local clergymen suggest they were among the leading opponents of the singing saloons. The Revd John Clay was a severe critic of the singing saloons and campaigned for reform and better education in sympathy with the temperance movement. The level of his concern was even mirrored in his annual report as chaplain of Preston Prison in 1842. 'Since these places are so overwhelmingly frequented it follows that sound education is becoming diffused.' The Revd Clay even allowed a prisoner in his early twenties to endorse his 1842 Annual Report with the inmate's own experiences of the Albion concert room in around 1840:

At such places there was singing and dancing and acting and all sorts of performances... I have tried to give over going to such places but there was always someone to ask me if I was not going to the concert... I was never fond of drink but the singing and dancing enticed me to go and I can say with some safety these places have been my ruin and I have no doubt they have been the ruin of many more... I think it would be a good thing if they were stopped. I have seen 500 or 600 at the [unnamed venue]. They are mostly young people, factory people, lawyers, clerks and all sorts of people. There are twelve persons in prisons now that I have seen there. I took seventeen watches altogether. I generally pawned them for one third their value at the playhouse and concert room.

Thus the prisoner appears to attribute his incarceration to drink and the handling of stolen goods in the concert room and theatre and the passage is testimony to the corrupting influences of the Albion's concert rooms upon him.

The prisoner's account reveals that prior to the Theatres Act of 1843, the music-hall performance was said to integrate 'singing and dancing and acting and all sorts of performances.' Significantly the Albion attracted '500 to 600, mostly young people, factory people, lawyers, clerks and all sorts of people.' The composition of the first Preston concert room audience integrated young working-class factory workers but was not their exclusive preserve, nor was it gender specific, with small numbers of the middle-class element such a lawyers and 'all sorts of people,' in attendance at the birth of music hall.

Interestingly, Charles Dickens probably makes a veiled reference to the Revd John Clay and the ruination of an inmate at Preston in his writings on Coketown in *Hard Times*:

> Then came the experienced chaplain of the jail, with more tabular statements, outdoing all the previous tabular statements and showing that the same people would resort to low haunts, hidden from the public eye, where they heard low singing and saw low dancing, and where A.B. aged 24 next birthday, and committed for eighteen months solitary, had himself said (not that he had ever shown himself particularly worthy of belief) his ruin began as he was perfectly sure and confident that otherwise he would have been a tip-top specimen.

In 1852 the Revd Clay gave evidence to a Select Committee on public houses when he distinguished between adults and young people in relation to their choice of venue: 'The adults ascribe their ruin to the beerhouses and public houses; the young ones ascribe their ruin as far as it goes, to the concert and dancing room.' Clay, like Livesey, was opposed to music hall because of its attraction for young people and their exposure to moral danger: 'The child rejected or outraged at home soon finds in the streets or fields companions in misery or idleness... then arises the inclination for debasing entertainment and it is plentifully supplied by low theatres and singing saloons.'

By 1865 many pubs, concert and dancing halls were patronised by the young working classes. A contemporary report in *The Preston Chronicle* stated:

> It must be confessed that the recreations in which the working classes can indulge are but few in number: the public house, the singing room, with its well puffed attraction, the dancing room and you have enumerated all the places in which he is a welcome guest... True there are temperance halls and of the latter we cannot speak too highly, but of the former (singing and dancing saloons) we cannot say much in the way of praise; taking the Preston hall as a specimen a dirtier or more unattractive place than which it would be difficult to find.[22]

The young cotton operatives were one significant group of workers who patronised Preston's concert rooms: 'At the Black Swan during January, 1865, seats were occupied by 60 or 70 lads and lassies of the cotton operative class and only three men were present.' The reporter claimed an alarmingly high number of young girls had been present as *filles publiques* or prostitutes. The simple and hedonistic form of the entertainment would have been seen by reformers as being part of this low moral tone and unsuitable for the young cotton operatives. 'Two coloured minstrels were dancing and a ventriloquist entered into dialogue with two young girls and questioned them through the mouthpiece of the doll about "nature's best handiwork – a lovely woman". The girls answered with unrepeatable expletives that were received with roars of laughter and delight by the audience!' This type of dialogue suggests a type of double entendre expressed in some singing saloons and concert halls.

It may be argued that these writers demonstrate moral panic over the composition of the working-class music hall. The tone of the above reports suggest that the Whig *Preston Chronicle* clearly aimed to further the temperance cause by bringing about the closure of drinking establishments and certain music halls with this type of propaganda. The working-class basis of music hall and the fact that it numbered young people and prostitutes in its audience were factors which inspired the attempts by temperance reformers, clergy and Nonconformists to influence the authorities to close down singing saloons, on the grounds that they were places of ill repute.

During 1868 a meeting was held in the Preston Temperance Hall to present the magistrates with a petition not to grant any more spirit licences on the grounds that the number of houses licensed (including music halls) was quite sufficient for the needs of the town. Typical of the temperance reformers' attacks is the thrust of an article written in 1870 by Thomas Walmsley, an original teetotaller: 'Much attention has of late been drawn to the desirability of public entertainments, with a view to checkmating the evils of the music saloons… One ill conducted public house with a singing room does an unspeakable amount of damage.'

Nationally many temperance reformers, especially Nonconformists, were suspicious of both theatres and music halls. 'We presume that nearly all our readers are opposed to the theatre,' wrote the *Weekly Record*, a leading temperance paper, on 8 November 1862. Attacks on the Manchester Palace Theatre took place at the time of its 1891 opening when the Wesleyans invoked 'the aid of the Almighty in a day of prayer to prevent its opening.'

Not everyone agreed with the tenor of the national out-and-out temperance attacks on music hall and a case for the embattled Manchester Palace was written in the following terms:

I wish to express my disgust at the tactics the Wesleyans are pursuing in their endeavour to defeat the license. I refused to sign the petition but as a shopkeeper I am well aware that many of my customers are Wesleyans and that my refusal will lose me trade. I hope the promoters will be successful because a well conducted music hall is sadly needed in Manchester.

The original 'Manchester Palace of Varieties' was officially opened on 18 May 1891, but without a licence to sell intoxicating liquor. The programme featured the ballet *Cleopatra*, and with Marie Lloyd topping the bill, the theatre was packed out.

There is little evidence of a tolerant approach from Preston's temperance reformers, whose tone was of condemnation if not moral outrage. A moral stance is expressed in 1876 by Chief Constable Oglethorpe in an address to the Preston Brewster Sessions in which he vigorously attacked music-hall culture, singling out the George in particular, then under the management of Martin Brown:

These places are resorted to by large numbers of young persons of both sexes and I am of the opinion that they are the first step on the road to ruin and disgrace for many young people. At one of these houses, the George Inn, Friargate, on a Saturday night may be found from 500 to 700 young persons of both sexes, from 200 to 300 of them apparently under the age of 16 years.

During the same week the concert-hall audience was reported to be a disproportionate ratio of 160 males to only 10 females, suggesting that on most occasions a male audience of young cotton operatives predominated. It is interesting to note that Oglethorpe's criticism is of the more refined George Music Hall, which suggests that the efforts of the social reformers to raise concerns over the moral welfare of young people were meeting with success, in terms of influencing the authorities.

Voice from the Gods

'Ladies and Gentlemen: There now follows a short intermission prior to a visit to the principal singing-room in Preston. I refer you to the theatre programme for further details but should add that the erotic performance to be exhibited is considered unsuitable for the faint-hearted. Those of a nervous disposition must leave the theatre forthwith or ruminate over the bare revelations of what is surely the first historical account of striptease in a Preston music hall which has been documented for posterity by clergy. I refer you to the Revd John Clay's *Annual Report* of 1850': [23]

A Visit to the Principal Singing-Room in Preston (1850)

Having frequently heard of the demoralising scenes to be witnessed in the principal singing room in this town, and their effects on society, we were determined to visit it and judge for ourselves. Our visit was made on a Saturday evening. The advertisements announced that the 'Illustrious Stranger,' would be performed; afterwards singing and dancing; to conclude with the 'Spare Bed.' On proceeding up the archway leading to the room, we passed several groups of very young boys; whose apparent poverty but not their will prevented their entrance. The price of admission is two pence or four pence. Desirous of seeing as much as we could, we paid four-pence. On receiving our tickets we went into the lower part of the room, and the sight which then presented itself baffles description. The performance had commenced and what with the 'mouthings' of the performers, the vociferous shouts, the maledictions, the want of sufficient light, and the smoke from about one hundred tobacco pipes, the effect was quite bewildering for a few minutes.

The room is oblong about 30 yards by ten and capable of holding with the galleries from 800 to 1,000 persons. One end is fitted up as a stage. The bar where the liquors are sold out is placed in the middle. The place between the bar and the stage is appropriated to juveniles or boys and girls from ten to fourteen years of age, of them there were not less than a hundred, they were by far the noisiest portion of the audience, and many of the boys were drinking and smoking. The compartment behind the bar appears to have been fitted up for the 'respectables,' the seats being more commodious. Leaving this lower part of the room we had to proceed up a dark staircase, (some parts being almost impassable owing to the crowds of boys and girls) to the lower gallery, which extends around three parts of the room. This gallery was occupied by the young of both sexes, from 14 years and upwards. To reach the top gallery we had to mount some more crazy stairs. This gallery is composed of two short side sittings and four boxes in the front. The occupants of these boxes are totally secluded from the eyes of the rest of the audience. They were occupied by boys and girls. From this gallery we had a good view of all that was passing in the room. There could not be less than 700 individuals present, and about one seventh of them females.

The pieces performed encourage resistance to parental control, and were full of gross innuendoes, 'double entendres,' heaving, cursing, emphatic swearing and incitement to illicit passion. Three fourths of the songs were wanton and immoral, and were accompanied by immodest gestures. The last piece performed was the 'Spare Bed', and we gathered from the conversation around, that this was looked for with eager expectation. We will not attempt to describe the whole of this abominable piece; suffice it to say that the part, which appeared most pleasing to the audience, was when one of the male performers prepared to go to bed. He took off his coat and waistcoat, unbuttoned his braces, and commenced unbuttoning the waistband of his trousers, casting mock-modest glances around him; finally he took his trousers off and got into bed. Tremendous applause followed this act. As the man lay in bed the clothes were pulled off; he was then rolled out of bed and across the stage, his shirt being up to the middle of his back. After this he walked up and down the stage, and now the applause reached its climax – loud laughter, shouting, clapping of hands, by both males and females, testified the delight they took in this odious exhibition. The piece terminated about 11 o'clock and many then went away. It is necessary to state that the man had on a flesh-coloured pair of drawers, but they were put on so that the audience might be deceived and some were deceived.

It needs little stretch of the imagination to form an opinion on what the conduct of these young people would be on leaving this place – excited by the drink which they have imbibed, their witnessing this vile performance – their uncontrolled conversation. We have heard many persons express their sorrow at the apparent increase in the number of prostitutes in this town, some ascribing it to one thing and some to another. Visit this place and a very palpable cause is manifest. It is the manufactory and rendezvous of thieves and prostitutes. We saw several boys who had recently been discharged from prison. The audience was composed entirely of young persons. The average age of the whole assembly would not be above the age of 17 years. We did not see during the evening half a dozen respectable working men. The audience consisted of that portion of society that demands our most special care and attention – the rising generation. Many of them we could tell, by their conversation, were regular visitors. Some of the boys and girls were enabled to follow the singers in their songs; they could tell the names of the performers, their salaries, and converse on their relative merits. We did not see one female whose modesty seemed shocked or offended, by anything done or said on the stage.

We left the room about 11 o'clock, and there remained between 200 and 300 persons, one fourth of whom would be juveniles. As we have said, the room contained on one period 700 spectators; but the entire number which visited it, during the night, must have reached 1,000. We have visited many singing rooms, both metropolitan and provincial, but for gross and open immorality, for pandering to the depraved tastes of an audience, for exciting the passions of the young, for sensual exhibitions, this place surpasses all. We left it with a firm conviction that we may build Mechanics' Institutes, erect and endow churches, increase the number of gospel Ministers, and improve our Prison Disciple, but while we tolerate this nuisance we labour in vain.

Since the above account was drawn up, a boy has been committed to the prison, to take his trial on several charges of felony – whom we saw taking a prominent part among the loud applauders of the spare bed.

CHARLES CASTLES AND AMOS WILSON

The above findings of Mssrs Castles and Wilson paint a sordid picture of an 1850 Preston singing saloon encapsulating evidence of the gender ratio and age of audiences; building structure (two tiers and boxes) and audience capacity; admission prices; alcohol provision and an account of the entertainment on offer featuring singers and what was probably an illegal sketch of the man in the *Spare Bed*. Whatever its faults, music hall had a strong appeal to the working classes and was the preferred option to the temperance hall, yet clearly there was a need for social and legal reform.

The Moral and Legal Response to the Victorian Music Hall

As well as expressing their condemnation in the strongest persuasive terms, those who promoted temperance and respectability knew from the beginning that alternative entertainments and leisure pursuits were needed if they were to win converts to their cause. Thus rational recreation was promulgated in Preston by an influential section of the town's middle-class leaders and temperance advocates. Based on the assumption that working-class people needed to be protected from their own weaknesses, the aim was to lure them away from leisure pursuits associated with alcohol consumption through superior and respectable counter-attractions.

Preston Corporation first enclosed 100 acres of Preston Moor as Moor Park as early as 1834. With further development of Miller and Moor Parks in the early 1860s the council aimed to provide recreational facilities and at the same time engage textile workers with employment in landscaping at the height of the Cotton Famine.

The Liberal members with their alliance to the Nonconformist and teetotal movement welcomed any move to lure the workers away from the pub environment. Education and self improvement were another side to the promotion of respectability; an issue referred to by the recorder of Preston, Joseph Catterall, during 1869 when he attacked the pub culture:

> There ought to be very stringent regulations as to prostitutes and persons of notoriously bad character being allowed to congregate together in these houses. Yet supposing that the best licensing system possible should be carried out, we should still be far from suppressing the vice of drunkenness and its too often criminal results. This can only be done by education, judiciously adapted to the wants of our populations.

The promotion of improvement through education as a counter-attraction was boosted with the opening of the Avenham Institute in October 1849. The main storey had a theatre, library, reading room, committee rooms, classrooms and a lecture theatre with capacity for 600 people. The subscriptions were 6s 6d a year and included access to a library of 1,500 books; these circulated at the rate of 300 a week. At the time of Dickens' visits, during the 'Great Lockout of 1853,' the institute was described as 'lifting the souls of impoverished cotton workers.'

In Preston education had only limited success in competing with the pub and music-hall culture. Questions arose concerning the success of counter-attractions and the level of education received. Clay (1852) said: 'The Avenham Institute does not do the good one would wish – it cannot rival the beer shops and public houses.' The continual growth of music hall for many years after the founding of the Avenham Institute is evidence of its limited success as an opposing attraction and as Joyce (1982) states: 'The education received in the Mechanics and Church Institutes, often amounted only to the teaching of basic reading and writing. The music hall, the sports stadium and the popular press triumphed over the mechanics' institute and the temperance society.' [24]

During the period of music-hall growth, reformers were persistent in their efforts to attract workers into what were perceived as worthy leisure pursuits. The concern to encourage rational recreation for the working classes embraced a whole range of counter-attractions, several of which were listed by Joseph Livesey in 1867. 'There are the mechanics' institute, newsroom, library, working men's club, gymnasium, lectures, temperance meetings, concerts and tea parties.' [25]

Concerts intended to counter the singing saloon were inspired by a meeting that took place on 15 October 1840, 'holden at the White Horse Inn in Preston', to initiate the Preston Choral Society and improve the musical taste in the town. There was also a moral aim: 'that no more places be opened to corrupt and ruin our young people.' From the 1840s onward, concerts and recitals were organised in different venues including the Corn Exchange and the Avenham Institute Theatre. Conjurers and jugglers were sometimes invited to provide

The Victorian splendour of Preston Public Hall. (Courtesy of the *Lancashire Evening Post*)

additional entertainment in the effort to offer an alternative to the pub and music hall. With the opening of the rebuilt public hall in Preston in 1882, musical and choral societies and orchestral concerts and oratorios were sustained as a feature of Victorian entertainment in the town. Captain J. Norwood presented his annual concerts with vocalists and maintained the orchestral tradition for over forty years.

Possibly as a consequence of the reformers' attacks on music hall, the Albion was closed in 1856 and transformed into the Spinners and Minders' Institute, capable of accommodating 500 persons. The premises were used by the Spinners' Institute until closure in 1882 when the total number of members was 740. Henry Solly, supported by the temperance movement, founded the working men's club and institute union in 1862 and a working men's club was established in Preston as early as 1863. Working men's clubs at first avoided both the provision of alcohol and music-hall entertainment and instead presented drama, poetry and occasional orchestral concerts including regular visits by Mr Norwood's Concert Band to Preston Conservative Club. The sale of beer on club premises first occurred in Preston clubs during 1868, prompting Livesey to suggest that they had failed in their principal aim of providing a counter-attraction to the public house. During the twentieth century, clubs offered a combination of live variety entertainment and alcohol that contradicted the basic philosophy of rational recreation by following the lead of the music hall, and overall there is little evidence that the clubs succeeded in drawing workers away from their drink.

A Music Hall 'Cop Out?'

The promotion of respectable forms of recreation led to music-hall proprietors adopting the rhetoric of respectability as a defensive strategy. There is evidence of programming that aimed to add refinement to the entertainment, and of propaganda from proprietors designed to counter possible condemnation from the temperance movement. Being aware that respectability was the criterion of social acceptability, music-hall proprietors tried to instil its values into existing audiences and thus attract larger audiences from the middle class by emulating the arguments of reformers:

> National Music Hall, at Wagon and Horses, Tithebarn Street – powerful attraction during the Whitsuntide holidays, Monday June 13th 1859 – change of company – mirth and music… elevating tendencies to promote the moral, social and intellectual progress of mankind, to excite kindly sympathy towards each other among all classes of society and to inspire those lofty sentiments which poetry and music convey.

Evidence of competition between the Church and music hall is provided in 1861, when the Wagon and Horses Music Hall drew on the appeal of religious music in a respectable programme: 'The proprietor has purchased an organ, on which there will be played a variety of Sacred Music every Sunday evening, commencing at half past six, and closing at ten o'clock.'

Respectability was at the forefront of advertising when Edward Blackoe opened the George Music Hall to capacity audiences of around 1,000 in November 1864. A lengthy press article extolled its virtues with slogans offering:

> Nothing but the strictest morality and respectability… A responsible door-keeper is stationed at the entrance to allow none to visit but orderly and well behaved persons, excluding boys and girls… Instructive mottoes are placed up on the walls impressing the reader with good and truthful maxims – 'moderation, a safe principle'; 'honesty is the best policy'; 'morality and prudence are much admired'; 'civility produces many friends'; 'no pains no gains'; and 'he who agrees with himself agrees with others'… There was nothing calculated to disgust or demoralise. On the contrary the audience, quiet and well behaved, consisted of respectable looking grown up people, not children, and apparently not a single *fille publique* was present.

John Blackoe opened the new King's Head Concert Hall in November 1870. Again, the importance of respectability in its promotion is evidenced by the following original quotation with three references to the word 'respectability' emphasised in the space of thirty-seven words as reported in *The Preston Chronicle*: 'The King's Head is the largest and most respectable in the town engaging first class talent worthy of the appreciation of a really respectable audience. Good ale and spirits, music, talent and respectable treatment always on hand.'

This type of propaganda reported in the Whig *Chronicle* show that temperance had a direct effect on how music hall was offered to the public and gives the impression that respectability was beginning to govern the tone of the music-hall industry in Preston. Although such claims should not be taken entirely at face value, the Blackoes probably made a concerted effort to instil good management to counter temperance attacks and rational recreation activities, and therefore music-hall proprietorship came to promote respectability.

The Theatre Royal, like the George, had to show a clear concern for propriety during its 1867 music-hall season:

> The prices of admission on the most reasonable terms to suit all classes of respectability; the entertainment to surpass anything yet attempted in Preston. Prices: centre boxes 1/6d,

side boxes 1/-, pit 6d, gallery 3d. Doors open 7 p.m., to commence at 7.30 p.m., to conclude 10 p.m., half price at 9 p.m. to boxes only. No boys under 16 years unless accompanied by parents, Children in arms not admitted, no disorderly characters. Police officers in attendance to maintain order, three months tickets obtainable with reasonable rates from the manager.

The efforts of reformers to expose the working classes to a respectable leisure and entertainment culture matching middle-class values can be seen to have been influential in Preston, especially in its moral concerns, as it prompted music-hall proprietors to promote respectability themselves. Respectability did not persuade drinking customers to forgo music hall but in this way it gradually moved away from being an essentially working-class form of entertainment and towards having a mass appeal. Social reform was only one aspect though, for throughout the period, temperance and political persuasions had their part to play in instilling a modicum of legal reform – as we will see in the next 'very pwopa performance.'

Political and Temperance Influences on Music Hall Reform: 'Yes and Very Pwopa.'
The United Kingdom Temperance Alliance was formed in 1853 and emerged as a potent political force. The success of the pubs and music halls gave rise to intense opposition with evidence of written attacks by reformers and defensive counter-measures taken by music-hall proprietors. Criticism alone did not satisfy reformers; they also demanded legal reform, which eventually contributed to the demise of Preston's pub music halls during the Victorian era.

As part of the movement towards greater control of music hall and based on the recommendations of Preston's Chief Constable, James Dunn, in 1864, the Watch Committee expressed their view on concert halls to the Home Office. 'It is desirable that no house, room, booth or other place within boroughs or other populous places should be kept or used for public dancing, music, dramatic or other public entertainment without a licence first obtained from the JPs having jurisdiction within the borough.' Nationally, the trend towards reform can be seen

THE NATIONAL MUSIC HALL, WAGGON AND HORSES INN, LORD-STREET, Will open for the winter season, on Saturday Evening, November 2nd, with a talented company of MALE and FEMALE VOCALISTS, and will be open every Monday, Tuesday, and Saturday Evenings, until further notice.

The Proprietor begs to inform his friends and the public in general that he has newly-decorated the hall, and made improvements for the comfort of visitors. He has also purchased an Organ, on which there will be played a variety of Sacred Music every Sunday Evening, commencing at half-past six, and closing at ten o'clock.

During 1861 the Wagon and Horses was dubbed 'the National Music Hall'.

in two Select Committee reports of 1852 and 1877, which enquired into the licensing of pubs, beerhouses, theatres and public places of entertainment, advocating closer police supervision, and expressing concerns over public morality.

The early teetotallers came from the Liberal/Radical Nonconformist section of society, and were backed by the Whig *Preston Chronicle*. Preston was, until 1945, a two-seat constituency, and one of the last to return two MPs. Most Nonconformists voted Liberal, while most Anglicans voted Conservative, but from the early days of the nineteenth century up to the 1830s the returns had been equally divided between Whigs and Tories. After 1840 the balance tipped towards the Liberals, but again became more equally divided between Liberal and Tory from 1852 -1859. During a crucial period of music-hall development the Conservatives held the two Preston seats (from 1859-1906). The influence of the drink lobby in Parliament together with Conservative dominance in local politics lent support to the brewing industry and the idea of licence applications, and thus assisted the growth of music hall in Preston. This favourable influence can be seen to be a factor in the pub music hall reaching its peak in the late 1860s and early 1870s.

In 1854, at a time when Preston was witnessing an expansion of the drinks and music-hall industries, over 50 per cent of the town's magistrates were cotton manufacturers and 67 per cent were Church of England Tories. Only 14 per cent of the magistrates were directly linked as members of the Preston Temperance Society. This Tory dominance of magistrates augured well for the publicans, since the alliance between Tories and the pub industry was evident. A correspondent referred to the partisan nature of magistrates at Preston in 1870, complaining about a disproportionate ratio in favour of Conservatives over Liberals, with fifteen Conservatives against only six Liberals appointed to the Preston Bench. The magistrates could not, however, avoid being affected by the level of temperance campaigning and public opinion, and adopted a policy of trying to stem the increase in the number of public houses and music halls. This is hardly surprising given the strength of the temperance campaign in Preston. Temperance opposition dominated the social conflicts around the halls and eventually countered the favourable influence of an alliance between Tories and the breweries.

During the 1870s there were moves afoot that would impact on music hall with the imposition of stringent licensing conditions for premises offering live entertainment, supported by one *Chronicle* newspaper correspondent using the light-hearted pseudonym 'Very Pwopa' in February 1871:

> Sir, A meeting will be held in the Corn Exchange on the 23rd in reference to the proposed government Public House Licensing Bill, when magistrates and Town Councillors are expected to be there. Yes, and very pwopa. Let us hope the conference, whilst denouncing and sending to smithereens the vulgar licensed public-houses and beershops, will pledge themselves to maintain inviolate the sanctity of the upper ten's wine cellars, bins, and vindegardes. Yes and very pwopa.

Very Pwopa's message is very clear and, despite the humorous annotations, reflects the level of public concern expressed at the forthcoming meeting by the Licence Amendment League into a proposed licensing bill at Preston Corn Exchange on the 23 February 1871. It was presided over by a leading clergyman, Archdeacon Hornby, and attended by the mayor, magistrates and local clergy. There were more attacks on singing saloons and it was proposed to reform the Liquor Licensing Law and to exercise tighter control over the sale of intoxicating liquor in any singing or dancing saloon or other place of amusement. This demonstrates that music halls in any form were now being specifically targeted for reform under the law in a concerted attack.

Lobbying of this kind and powerful campaigning by the temperance movement brought improved licensing laws in 1872 governing licensing, opening hours and policing measures, which the Gladstone government passed with Conservative support. The strength of opposition to music hall can still be seen, however, in comments made in 1877 by the Chief Constable of Preston, J. Oglethorpe, to the House of Lords' Commissioners on Intemperance: 'There is one evil in public houses as far as morality is concerned and that is having concert rooms and dancing rooms attached to them.' This attitude, together with the pressure of petitions to magistrates and police, was to meet with some success in Preston by influencing the adoption of legislation that was to contribute to the ultimate demise of the Victorian pub music hall.

Before the 1850s it had only been in London and the area within a twenty-mile radius that a separate music and dancing licence had been required in addition to a liquor licence. During 1851, Birmingham introduced separate music licences and, elsewhere in the provinces, a similar trend of local Acts affecting the existence of the pub music halls gradually followed suit. Local autonomy over the control of licensing for music halls was eventually incorporated into Section 129 of the Preston Improvement Act, 1880, which was partially manifested through the strength of opposition to music hall and the possible need to placate the temperance cause. The Local Government Act, 1888, unified existing local laws and made national music-hall licensing compulsory. Like the majority of councils, Preston delegated duties back into the hands of the magistrates, who were already exercising their powers under Section 129 of the Improvement Act.

Act Two – The Edwardian Music Hall

Scene One: Edwardian Variety and the 'Battle for the King's Palace'

Voice from the Gods

'Notice from the manager: For the convenience of second house patrons of boxes, circle, and orchestra stalls, the theatre waiting room will be open at 7.30 p.m. Read all about the events that led to the opening of the Royal Hippodrome in 1905, an event that ended a sixteen-year hiatus in music-hall provision in Preston and preceded the building of three variety theatres in the town.'

As a distinct genre, variety was the most widespread form of urban entertainment throughout the Victorian and Edwardian eras, but thereafter it began to take on other entertainment styles, notably revue. Variety can be defined as a series of attractions or 'turns' unconnected by any theme. In Great Britain it was originally known as music hall, though the two terms are often used interchangeably. The American form was known as Vaudeville.

The London Pavilion was reconstructed in 1885; Stuart and Park, writing in 1895, saw this event as having, 'inaugurated a fresh era in music-hall history'. Nationally, the number of variety theatres grew, and in 1899 *The Era Almanac* listed 226 variety halls in the provinces. The 1890s was a decade of particular success for music hall and might be described as the golden years of British music hall when all classes were attracted to the variety halls. Consideration will first be given to the lack of a regular music hall in Preston at the turn of the century, when the town's population had increased to 112,989 by 1901, for this was atypical of a populous urban area. Preston's variety theatres were built between 1905 and 1913, towards the end of the national music-hall boom which lasted until the outbreak of the First World War. Thus there is a paradox: a town that, in other respects, broadly follows the national and regional trends in music-hall development had no new music halls built and, so far as can be ascertained, none sustained during the 1890s. Circumstantial and direct evidence suggests that opposition from magistrates, governing both building construction as well as the conduct of the premises, led to the eventual closure of the town's Victorian music halls.

The hiatus in Preston's music hall was probably the result of a combination of factors. Among these, local autonomy governing the enforcement of licensing was significant in the reduction of the music hall. The licence issued under Section 129 of the Preston Improvement Act, 1880, was valid for twelve months, with terms and conditions, for the regulation of public dancing, music, and other public entertainment and had to be issued whether or not the premises were licensed for intoxicants; in 1876 and 1880 the combined total of public houses and beerhouses licensed for music and entertainment was around thirty-one and eighteen respectively. During 1882, after the introduction of the Act, *The Era* lists only the Gaiety, the George and the

King's Head as presenting music hall, indicating an immediate post-1880 reduction of music and dancing licences. During the next decade, however, each of these venues would close.

The decline of the pub concert hall also coincided with tighter controls on licensing initiated prior to the Improvement Act by the effect of the Metropolitan Management and Building Act, 1878, governing building and safety regulations. The Act, adopted nationally, required a Certificate of Suitability for a proscenium wall, which divided the stage from the auditorium, and a heavy iron safety curtain, but smaller concert halls could not take its weight. The economy of the halls was also seriously affected by a requirement that bars be separated from the auditoria with a consequential reduction in alcohol consumption. The new legislation caused some 200 halls unable to meet the new standards to close. This was no less true in Preston, where its impact was felt by the proprietor of the Gaiety Music Hall. From the time of its 1882 opening it was delicately balanced in terms of its financial viability, as is borne out by its short life of only six years as a music hall whilst managed by a lessee, Harry Yorke.

The manager of the Theatre Royal successfully opposed an application by Yorke of the Gaiety Music Hall for a dramatic licence as early as 1885. During 1888, Yorke was paying an annual rent of £320 a year but incurred debts to carry out the necessary alterations to the Gaiety that had been demanded by the inspecting magistrates. As an interim measure, Yorke was granted a three-month music and dancing licence before being granted a dramatic licence. During October 1888, the theatre reopened as a drama theatre and with a change of name: 'Mr Harry Yorke's Gaiety Theatre, will in future be known as the Prince's Theatre and Opera House and will be used only for dramatic purposes.'

The problems of the Gaiety show the difficulties facing concert hall managers, who struggled to afford the expense of extensive alterations at the time of their annual licence application. However, the improved legislation did not prevent a serious fire at the former Preston music hall in 1900. This resulted in the rebuilding of the proscenium and stage area before it reopened in December 1900 with capacity for 2,500.

The Clarence, Grimshaw Street was also one of Preston's last concert rooms to close. The undated programme from the Clarence reproduced on page 10 shows, through the mention of the Preston North End player Belger, that it was printed around 1883. By now the refreshment token had been superseded, but the inducement of free music hall was still being funded by the advertised choice of alcohol and cigars on sale in the auditorium. The programme also illustrates the moderate style of locally based entertainment on offer and claims that, 'it was the place to spend a convivial hour', drop in to sample the programme. Curiously, 'children in arms were not admitted unless brought by someone.'

The decline in music hall in Preston was such that by November 1889, the George was advertising in a local newspaper as being: 'The only music hall in town. Special attractions. Concert tonight at 7.30 p.m.,' lending support to the view that the other music halls had ceased to exist; in any event, the George was demolished in a scheme to widen Friargate in 1895.

Many theatres were built both in London and the provinces during the Edwardian era. There were over 260 theatres open throughout Britain in 1901, illustrating the flourishing state of the theatrical industry. Liverpool had eight theatres, Manchester and Glasgow had seven apiece. The anomaly of the lack of a significant music-hall presence in Preston between around 1889 and 1905 becomes more apparent when it is contrasted with other Lancashire towns. Burnley, for example, had two drama theatres: the Victoria, and the Gaiety Theatre. The continuity of Burnley's music-hall industry in the 1890s is illustrated by the construction of its first purpose-built music hall, 'The Empire,' which opened in October 1894 and had capacity for 2,500. The Empire was unchallenged as a variety theatre until 1908 when the Palace Hippodrome, with 2,000 seats, opened in the centre of town in December 1907.

LONDON PAVILION 6^{D.}

PROPRIETORS : THE LONDON PAVILION LTD.

MANAGER : FRANK GLENISTER.

Under the direction of CHARLES B. COCHRAN

"DOUGLAS FAIRBANKS

in

ROBIN HOOD"

Programme

Extracts from the Rules made by the Lord Chamberlain.—1.—The name of the actual and responsible **Manager** of the Theatre must be printed on every playbill. 2.—The Public can leave the Theatre at the end of the performance by all exit and entrance doors, which must open outwards. 3.—Where there is a fireproof screen to the proscenium opening it must be lowered at least once during every performance to ensure its being in proper working order. 4.—Smoking is permitted in the auditorium. 5.—All gangways, passages and staircases must be kept free from chairs or any other obstructions, whether permanent or temporary.

Above: The Prince's Theatre (formerly the Gaiety), Tithebarn Street. Beyond is the Regent Ballroom and King's Palace Theatre. (Courtesy of the Harris Reference Library, Preston)

Left and opposite: Theatres such as the London Pavilion (1885) and the Metropolitan (which opened in 1862 and closed in 1962) represented a new generation of variety theatres staging generic music-hall acts.

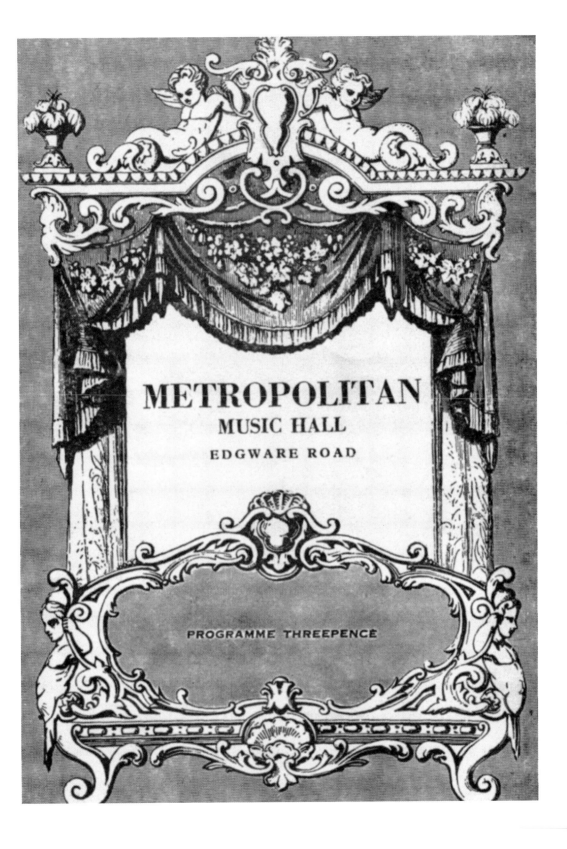

METROPOLITAN
MUSIC HALL
EDGWARE ROAD

PROGRAMME THREEPENCE

Two other Lancashire textile towns, Bolton and Blackburn, each had at least one legitimate theatre and purpose-built music hall at the turn of the century. At Bolton (population 115,002 in 1891), the rebuilt Victoria Theatre of Varieties operated as a music hall from 1882 and so did the Grand Cirque, opened in 1894. The Empire Theatre of Varieties opened in 1908 and became the Hippodrome. At Blackburn (population 120,064 in 1891), the Prince's Theatre opened in around 1890 and was rebuilt as the New Prince's Theatre in 1906. It was renamed the Grand in December 1931 and closed as a variety theatre in 1956. The Palace Music Hall opened on 11 December 1899 'with a first class variety bill.' It reopened as part of McNaughten circuit in September 1900.

Alternative Late Victorian Entertainment in Preston

By 1882, music-hall capacity in Preston was reduced to an estimated 4,500 seats comprising capacity at the 'The Gaiety' (2,000) 'The George', (1,000) the King's Head (1,000) and the Clarence (about 500). Rational recreation offered alternative forms of leisure, usually served by the philanthropic interests of the town. Alternative entertainment included both civic and private establishments, representing a formidable challenge to music hall.

In Preston the drama theatre, concert hall, travelling circus, Victorian Pleasure Garden and legitimate theatres were popular with the late Victorian and Edwardian audiences and filled the void of music-hall entertainment during the period up to 1905. This combination of alternative popular entertainment and increased licensing regulations may have forestalled syndicate interest during the 1880s and '90s. The Theatre Royal had capacity for 1,700 seats while the two concert halls, the public hall and the Guild Hall, had capacity for a total of 4,564 seats. The Temperance Hall had 800 seats for miscellaneous entertainment. In addition, there were an unspecified number of seats at the permanent and visiting circuses: a total estimated capacity of over 6,500 seats (excluding the travelling circuses) suggests a strong reason why music hall did not prosper during the 1880s.

Walton acknowledges that, 'what emerges is the sheer extent and range of commercial entertainment provision in the late Victorian and Edwardian cotton towns of Lancashire, building on and expanding from firm mid-Victorian foundations, and reaching almost all levels of working-class society.'[26]

The travelling circus and menagerie regularly visited Preston throughout the Victorian era. OHMY's Grand New Circus came to town in March 1884. The name OHMY was derived from its proprietor Joseph Smith, who as a circus bungee jumper was in the habit of shouting 'oh my'; hence the name of his travelling circus. The circus occupied a site on the west side of the railway station in Pitt Street that was to be displaced by the building of County Hall by the turn of the century. The *Preston Guardian* extolled the performance and the new building, advertising:

One of the best companies now in England, consisting of no less than 26 traditional circus acts including performing horses, ponies, mules, donkeys, goats, dogs, monkeys, pigeons and the smallest pony in the world. Foreign and British artists included Madam Cooke, from Barnum's Circus, Mons. Syllvester, 'the great somersault rider', Miss Louisa, 'the great French rider' and seven clowns acts including 'the people's jester… The beautiful new building, the best ever erected in Preston constructed from designs of Mr OHMY, splendidly decorated, comfortably seated, carpeted and well lit-up with gas. The circus is arranged with the same style as the grand Paris Circus with beautiful boxes, cosy pit, extensive promenade and smoking lounge, and one of the most comfortable galleries in England. Open every evening, Saturday at 2.30 p.m. stalls 3/-, box's 2/-, pit 1/-, promenades 6d. gallery 3d. Season ticket one guinea, children under ten and public after 9 o'clock – half price – except gallery.

Suburban Victorian pleasure gardens gained national popularity and were often served by the railway and local tramway network. Tramcars were not only an important stimulus to the social and economic development of the town's outer suburbs but also meant that the public could now attend the out-of-town entertainment as well as the new music halls of the Edwardian era. The newly established Preston Pleasure Gardens, New Hall Lane, had widespread appeal and were accessed by rail and tramcar: 'Tramcars from all the railway platforms, direct to the (pleasure garden) gates, every few minutes.' In addition to live entertainment there was a dancing pavilion, sports facilities and a zoological garden. Over 200 birds and animals representing 100 species were accommodated in the zoo. The popularity of the pleasure gardens was reflected on Sunday 20 August 1884 when 2,853 people visited the attraction.

Throughout the 1880s Preston Pleasure Gardens featured varied entertainment including circus and music-hall artists, some of whom had appeared at the Gaiety Temperance Theatre of Varieties in 1880. During Easter 1885 there was a grand fête:

> Special engagement of Mons Descombes and Madame Laura – will introduce his wonderful globe performance. Introducing juggling with tops, knives, torches, flags, balls, plates and finishing with balancing a monster full rigged ship of war on his chin and firing a volley of 48 guns at the same time. 'Madame Laura', without exaggeration the perfect and graceful lady – invisible wire equilibrist and manipulator – will perform some daring and extraordinary feats consisting of Japanese balancing, juggling and other evolutions. The gardens will be illuminated each evening with Chinese lanterns and coloured lights. At 9 p.m. a magnificent display of fireworks. Admission 6d each. Good Friday and Easter Sunday, 3d. Children half price.

'OHMY's Great Circus' played at the pleasure gardens in June 1889. Victorian pleasure gardens became a fashionable phenomenon throughout the country but had to compete with the growing number of established municipal parks with free access. The life of the Preston Pleasure Gardens, after opening in 1877, was short, and after the zoo closed in 1885 the gardens were sold in 1889.

A visit during November 1889 of 'Quaghens and Allen's Grand Circus, Corporation Street' had capacity audiences despite relatively high admission prices of 3s, 2s, 1s, 6d and 3d, suggesting its likely appeal to most classes of society. Over a one-month period it was claimed that the Christmas pantomime presented by the circus – an equestrian version of *Cinderella* – attracted 37,000 people. Such was the immense popularity of the circus in 1889 that there is a suggestion of a niche being filled with this popular entertainment genre; this success is also illustrative of a demand for live entertainment, an impression which is reinforced by the recollections of Pye in describing late Victorian entertainment in 1945: 'The memories of exciting entertainment as for instance OHMY's big wooden circus building and all for a penny for children on Saturday afternoons. Then later on Buffalo Bill's gigantic Wild West Show.'

Many distinguished soloists and musicians featured in concert performances at the Guild Hall, the original Corn Exchange and its successor the Public Hall of 1882. In December 1871 there was a performance by 'The Queen's Minstrels said to be the only company of Negro Comedians, Vocalists, and Dancers patronised by the Queen and recognised as the original and legitimate Christy's Minstrels.' Brass band concerts were very popular during the late nineteenth century and there was a balloon ascent in Moor Park during the Queen's Jubilee on the 26 June 1897; by complete contrast, a performance by Clara Butt on the 21 November 1900 exemplifies the calibre of artists appearing at the turn of the century: 'Miss Clara Butt made her appearance at Preston, and was given a splendid reception.' Admission prices were stalls 4s, gallery 3s, second area seats 2s 6d or 1s.

Programme of Dame Clara Butt's international tour, which included Preston.

Where other towns had both music hall and circus, Preston stands out as lacking the former during the late Victorian era; we will probably never know exactly why this highly specific pattern developed in Preston. After the closures of the Gaiety and the George, music hall was not revived in the town until the syndicates took an interest during the Edwardian era and brought Preston back in line with the national pattern of growth.

Ovation for W.H. Broadhead & Sons

It was in the 1890s that that Moss, Thornton and Stoll began building Empires, Palaces and Hippodromes throughout England. The 'Gaiety Theatre' and rebuilt Theatre Royal set the foundations for the new architecturally designed people's emporia. The Broadhead syndicate, a Manchester-based firm, had the financial resources to exploit the opportunity that a town without a clearly recognisable music hall presented, and extended their empire from the Manchester area by opening two music halls in Preston: the belated Royal Hippodrome in 1905 and the King's Palace Theatre in 1913. The King's Palace, Preston, was the last of the theatres to be built by William Henry Broadhead's building firm. Part of the company's philosophy was that in the case of poor box-office returns their theatres could be redesigned for use as factories. However, neither the Hippodrome nor the King's Palace saw this type of adaptation and both survived as music halls until the 1950s.

The Broadhead family played a major role in the establishment of music hall in north-west England. William Henry Broadhead was born in Smethwick, (Staffs) in 1848 and entered the building trade at the age of fifteen. After meeting and marrying Mary Ann Birch in Manchester, he founded his own building firm with a head office in Tib Street, Manchester. In 1883, for health reasons, he moved to a 'famous seaside town called Blackpool, noted for fresh air and fun.' Three years later he took over the Prince of Wales Baths next to the Prince of Wales Theatre, which was managed by Thomas Sergenson, who opened the Grand Theatre in the resort in 1894. This was about the same time that another famous building, Blackpool Tower, was opened. The baths' site eventually became the Palace Variety Theatre, Cinema and Ballroom, but sadly it has been since demolished.

William Henry had four daughters and two sons, William (Willie) Birch Broadhead and Percy Baynham Broadhead. The Broadhead theatrical business really began when Willie managed to persuade his father to invest his capital in a theatre in Manchester. He earmarked sites for his theatres and the first theatre to be built was the Royal Osborne Theatre, Oldham Road, Manchester, which opened on the 13 April 1896. It was followed by the construction of fourteen theatres in Ashton-under-Lyne, Bury, Eccles, Liverpool, Manchester, Preston and Salford. In 1909 he opened the Palais-de-Danse at Ashton-under-Lyne and in the same year acquired the Winter Gardens, Morecambe. Three years later he purchased the Lyceum theatre, Eccles, later renamed the Crown. Both Preston theatres were part of the portfolio of seventeen Broadhead halls of entertainment – fourteen theatres and one dance hall built, and two theatres purchased, between 1896 and 1913, representing the glory days of variety.

The Broadhead theatre circuit was based in north-west England and was known to artists as the 'bread and butter' tour. (Courtesy of Major A. Burt Briggs)

William Birch was the inspiration behind the design of most of the theatres, and he employed an architect, a Mr J.J. Allen, to interpret his ideas. Frank Matcham, the renowned theatre architect who designed the extant Grand Theatre, Blackpool, influenced the style of architecture and interior design, and the theatres were generally built at a cost of between £9,000 and £11,000. The performer Percy Honri once said that 'W.H. Broadhead & Sons were builders of theatres rather than bidders for theatres someone else had built'. Alert and cheerful, William Birch Broadhead would drop in at any one of the performances at some point in the evening, but tragically, in 1907, he caught a cold and died at the age of thirty-four years. Percy Baynham Broadhead then managed the business with his father, and later with his own son, Percy Baynham Broadhead Junior.

As a family they displayed foresight by reacting to change. Their concept of respectability meant no vulgarity; they aimed to bring greater diversity of programming with 'dramatic productions of an uplifting moral nature', for working-class audiences in variety theatres at prices they could afford. The Broadhead Repertory Players performed across the circuit. Melodrama was staged at the Royal Osborne Theatre, Manchester (1895), Metropole (1898) and Grand Junction (1901). The Hulme Hippodrome and adjoining Grand Junction Music Hall were built as a 'vast palace of amusement for Hulme residents' and it was from adjoining offices that the Broadheads managed their entertainment business while anxious to cater for the big following for variety. William Henry Broadhead knew how to make money and toured his theatres in a Daimler limousine. Every morning he scrutinised the previous day's takings from all his theatres in special envelopes that were ceremoniously opened with a special paper knife by his grandson. Prices were kept down to those prevailing before the war and ranged from tuppence to a shilling. As the public got what they wanted there was no need for them to go to the city centre for an evening's entertainment.

A problem for the audience in 1905 was the system of 'early doors'. Many 'pit-ites', having taken the advice of the commissioners calling out 'this way to early doors', had moved over to that queue and paid a little extra to get into the theatre early to get the best seats – only to find that it had not been necessary as the auditorium was not yet full. It was suggested that all extra charges should be abolished and that the price of a theatre seat should include the cloakroom fee – thus going someway towards persuading ladies with tall hats to deposit them in the cloakrooms so as not to impair the view of the stage.

The Broadheads grasped that dramatic productions and a range of eclectic entertainment, including variety, was a marketable proposition. Their motto for variety interest was 'make it quick, clean, smart and bright'. The average wage of artists during the Edwardian period would be about £5-10 per week, and after paying for fares and living expenses they would not have had much cash left over. Broadhead's talent scout, Ernest Simms, had the job of engaging artists while watching their performances. If suitable, they were booked with a wage that was guaranteed while they toured the Broadhead circuit. The syndicate engaged acrobats, comics, glamorous dancing girls, magicians, singers, and a plethora of music-hall entertainers on what was affectionately known as 'the bread and butter circuit': this was because regular bookings did not produce the high wages of the Moss Empires, Stoll and other more prestigious theatre circuits.

Preston's expanding population and potential for renewed music-hall resurgence no doubt gave optimism to theatrical promoters and entrepreneurs. In the years leading up to 1914, theatres of variety dedicated to the ideal of family entertainment meant that the industry moved from being a local, largely class-based business in the hands of individual entrepreneurs, to a more centralised, increasingly respectable mass entertainment industry. The new Edwardian theatres of Preston established far-reaching changes in the cultural outlook of both the working and middle classes. Gone were the poor people's pub music halls, and by the time of the First World War even variety was being superseded by other rival entertainment styles, notably cinema.

Three Variety Theatres for Preston

During 1905 the Broadhead slogan of 'taking amusement and entertainment to the people at prices to reach the multitude' certainly had relevance to Preston in filling a void for music hall. William Henry Broadhead purchased 1,568 square yards of land and property in the area of Friargate/Black Horse Yard for £1,905 in 1903, and a further area of 753 square yards for £4,700 in 1904. Plans for the Royal Hippodrome were submitted to Preston Corporation on 7 May 1904. They were accepted, and building commenced almost immediately by Broadhead's Manchester building firm. The Royal Hippodrome opened after just eight months of building work; commencing on the 16 January 1905, it was managed by J. Freeman, who came from Broadhead's Queen's Park Hippodrome, Manchester. A final inspection of the premises took place on the 14 January 1905 when Mr W.P. Park, the chairman of the Inspection Committee, complimented Mr Broadhead on his enterprise and, after Mr. Broadhead agreed to some minor changes, a licence was granted. That night the theatre was thrown open for inspection by the general public and many thousands of Prestonians passed through the entrance. Monday 16 January brought blizzards, but this did not prevent the formal opening matinée performance playing to a full house with standing room only. The orchestra played the National Anthem and, as the stage was revealed, a hearty round of cheers resounded throughout the house.

The type of enthusiasm generated for the opening indicates that Broadhead was fulfilling a definite need. According to the *Lancashire Daily Post*:

> It certainly filled a long-felt gap in the town's entertainment provision…Time and again has a thoroughly up to date music hall and variety theatre been promised for Preston but it was not until some eight or nine months ago that definite arrangements for the construction of such a

Friargate with the façade of the Royal Hippodrome, *c.* 1905. (Courtesy of the *Lancashire Evening Post*)

building was brought to the notice of the public. A most substantial and pretty Hippodrome is certainly a decided acquisition.

The Hippodrome was lit by gas and electricity, which meant that safety provisions and fire inspections had to be rigorously enforced. The theatre exits facilitated that a 'full house' could be emptied in three minutes. An exceptionally large stage was fitted with a fireproof curtain and the lighting was arranged so that there was little danger of fire. Patent sprinklers were another a feature of the building. Thus, the Broadhead syndicate was able to meet more stringent regulations than those that the Gaiety had struggled to meet seventeen years before.

The Hippodrome is evidence of provision for a respectable Edwardian audience; at the same time, it attempted to reach the widest audience. The style of classical architecture and the private boxes at the Hippodrome were aimed at attracting a wide cross-section of the public:

> So far as the interior is concerned there is abundant evidence that no expense has been spared. The proscenium is in Ionic style with Renaissance panels and on each side are statues representing repose and silence, supported by brackets, imitative of the heads of satyrs. On each side is a handsomely furnished private box. All the main walls are furnished with rich crimson art paper which harmonises extremely well with the gold and white used in other decorations... All 2,500 seats command a fine view of the stage and a spacious waiting room was provided for the benefit of the second house patrons.

In contrast to the old pub concert halls, variety theatres were now more like the nationally established lavish theatres for drama.

The Royal Hippodrome, Preston, shortly before demolition, c. 1958. (Courtesy of Harris Reference Library, Preston)

The Empire Theatre, Preston, *c.* 1911. The complex included the extant Empire Hotel and was situated at the junction of Church Street and Tithebarn Street. (Drawing by C. Dodding)

The growing culture for music hall inspired a local entrepreneur and architect, Edwin Bush, to follow Broadhead's lead by building the Empire Theatre in 1911 with integrated shops on Church Street and chambers on three upper floors as well as the Empire Hotel in Tithebarn Street. Edwin Bush offered seats at the Empire priced between 4d and 1s 6d in 1911, compared with the Royal Hippodrome prices of 2s in the circle, 1s in the stalls, and 3d in the pit. It would seem that the period between the opening of the Empire in 1911 and the building of a second Broadhead theatre, the King's Palace, in 1913 was the time when Edwardian music hall was most economically successful in Preston. A total of three variety theatres by 1913 (for a population of 117,088) meant that they could expect to be profitable, as managers assumed that about one-third of the local population could be deemed potential customers.

The Empire Music Hall matched Preston's Hippodrome in having an audience capacity of 2,500. On the opening night, the 22 May 1911, many were unable to gain admission. A full description of the theatre was reported in *The Era*:

> The cost of the whole scheme is £65,000 and the venture is both bold and praiseworthy. The design of the theatre is in the Renaissance style of Louis XIV. There is a view of the stage from every part of the house. Entrance to the stage from the street is so ample in width and height that a motorcar, fire engine or 'coach and four' could drive straight across the stage in full view of the audience… The proscenium is flanked by two Georgian stage boxes… Each tier of boxes is crowned with an ornamental dome in line with the circle and gallery.

Left and opposite: Two views of the King's Palace theatre showing the main entrance in Old Vicarage, and the theatre as seen from Tithebarn Street. (Courtesy of Harris Reference Library, Preston)

The Era also describes the forms of entertainment planned: 'With the ever popular variety performance the management also intends to stage musical comedy, pantomime and grand opera at suitable periods. A determined effort is to be made to exclude rigidly from all performances that bugbear of the variety stage, doubtful humour, and to present at all times clean, wholesome amusement of the highest quality obtainable.'

The opening of Broadhead's King's Palace, Tithebarn Street on the 6 February 1913 gave Preston three purpose-built variety theatres offering respectable music hall and other forms of entertainment to a wide spectrum of Edwardian society. The building was described in *The Era* in February 1913:

> The building from the exterior, though neat in design and imposing in size, the King's Palace calls for no special eulogium…The auditorium is a delightful scheme of cream and gold in Louis XIV style crowned with a magnificent roof in fibrous plaster…The proscenium is a bold opening with gold and cream pilaster frame, flanked by sienna marble columns and two roomy stage boxes en suite, from which spring the bold curve of the circle…The stage itself is equipped with every modern contrivance and with a clear depth of 36' and width of over 70' and a lift of 50' will accommodate the most exigent of shows. From every seat a clear view of the stage is unobstructed by pillars of any kind… It is no secret that the proprietor consider the new house the 'best ever', either in the provinces or in town… One singular feature of the new house is that no provision has been made for pictures or for refreshment bars, a significant fact in view of Mr Broadhead's long connection with popular entertaining.

The Battle for the King's Palace

As we have seen, the opening of the Empire attracted favourable comment from the local press, but when the King's Palace Theatre opened on the 6 February 1913 there was serious opposition from other theatre owners on the grounds of over provision. The King's Palace was claimed

to be an embarrassing addition to the town's entertainment venues. Preston already had two music halls and two theatres: the Empire and the Royal Hippodrome and the Theatre Royal and the Prince's respectively. The capacity of the Hippodrome was 2,500; the Empire 2,500; the Theatre Royal 1,700; and the Prince's theatre 2,500. By 1913, Preston also sustained a total of twelve cinemas in the town. This gave an average of 40,000 theatre patrons per week excluding the cinema provision. Therefore the financial basis of Edwardian music hall in Preston was not entirely secure, especially after the opening of the second Broadhead theatre in February 1913, with total capacity for about 3,000. This, together with the emergence of cinema in the town, lends support to Bailey's view: 'By 1912 music hall was well into over production and reduced profits.'[27]

On the 3 February 1913, William Henry Broadhead applied to Preston Borough Court for licences to operate under the Theatre Act of 1843, and a Music, Singing and Dancing Licence to operate under the Preston Improvement Act of 1880, in respect of the new King's Palace Theatre. Counsel for Broadhead argued from the outset that the opposition was purely a trade dispute, submitting that his client was a suitable person to hold the licences as he was an established theatre owner whose new building met all of the safety requirements of the London County Council. Counsel for the owner of the Prince's said that, 'In the interests of fair play the licence should not be granted. The result of competition amongst the theatres would be the survival of the one with the longest purse.' The owners of the Empire Theatre and Theatre Royal jointly argued that not one of Preston's theatres realised a decent return on the capital invested in them. The owner of the Theatre Royal stated that, 'my house has suffered with the opening of the Empire and the Royal Hippodrome should be closed to compensate for the opening of the King's Palace.'

Under cross-examination Broadhead pointed out that the Hippodrome was the first music hall built in Preston and was built six years before the Empire opened. He refused to disclose the Royal Hippodrome's profitability, arguing that the theatres and cinemas were crowded on Mondays and Saturdays and sometimes on Thursdays. He told the court that Vaudeville shows would not be put on at the Hippodrome and the Palace in the same week. Despite the opposition and the distinct possibility of over provision, Broadhead got his licence for the vast 2,600-seat King's Palace venue with room for another 400 standing. The publicity gained by the opposition to the granting of a licence resulted in two bumper houses for the opening night – a variety night – only three days after the licence was granted and is illustrative of the popular approval of Broadhead's enterprise.

The foregoing shows that during the period between 1905 and 1913, Preston's music-hall patrons were adequately catered for, particularly with the provision of the King's Palace, but clearly there were doubts about its economic viability. These doubts were justified when, ironically, the expansion of the circuit and economics of running three competing music halls and two drama theatres in Preston led to the King's Palace itself becoming a full-time cinema from 1917, at a time when cinema was usurping the role of the variety theatres in Preston.

There seems little vindication for Broadhead's economic wisdom in opening a vast variety theatre at the time when theatrical provision had reached saturation point in 1913, though it may also be said that his over-optimism is characteristic of the time: 'In terms of numbers of buildings and audience size, variety reached its apotheosis in the period from 1910-1914.'[28]

Voice from the Gods
'Remember: Dramatic productions of an uplifting moral nature for the working classes at prices they can afford. Make it quick, clean, smart and bright.' W.H.B. (The Management)

Respectable Audiences and Twice-Nightly Performances
By 1905, the time of the opening of Preston's Royal Hippodrome, audiences were increasingly bound by the behavioural constraints of respectability. The middle classes took to visiting the halls when music halls were turned into variety theatres to make them more attractive to them. Elsewhere in similar sized Lancashire textile towns, the trend for music hall to adopt an image of Edwardian respectability is illustrated in a speech given by Frank Macnaughten at the opening of the Burnley Palace Hippodrome in 1908:

I am often asked why I call my halls, Palaces and Hippodromes. This is to draw a distinction between the old music hall of the past, frequented by men only, and the new Vaudeville entertainment of the present day, to be patronised by women and children... The old music hall is in the transition stage from the singing room to the new Vaudeville Variety theatre.

Indeed, Macnaughten's slogan heralded the respectability of variety, as 'Theatres of Variety dedicated increasingly to the ideal of family entertainment.'

The aim of attracting the widest possible respectable audience can be seen in what was expected of Broadhead's staff at the Hippodrome, who had to be especially clean and respectably dressed and live up to manager Walter Hume's catchphrase 'on the ball'. Before opening he paraded all the staff who dealt with the public and inspected their hands, nails and general appearance. He maintained that the box office and programme sellers' hands, faces and hairstyles must be up to the standards expected by patrons at that time. Being without a music hall, Preston cannot provide evidence of audience composition and management during the 1890s, but thereafter Broadhead's policy provides some evidence of the ongoing trend towards respectability.

The company maintained that the respectable citizen could take his wife and children to any of its productions, find them free from vulgarity and at a price well within his means. Admission prices were meant to cater for all classes through the provision of private boxes for the well-to-do and the segregation of the pit and gallery from the stalls and dress circle. In 1905 the seating at the Hippodrome was said to be well-arranged and of luxurious character with prices ranging from 3d in the pit to 2s for box and circle seats. Respectability was the keynote for all classes, as can be seen in the emphasis on: 'Absolute detached lavatories for ladies and gentlemen throughout the theatre.'

The revived music hall of the twentieth century undoubtedly saw managers increasingly attracting the middle classes by dispelling the public-house image, albeit there was to be less of the intimacy between performers and audience that was so much enjoyed by the Victorians. To meet increased costs and profitability the twice-nightly arrangement was introduced in London and Liverpool in around 1885 to raise the productivity of performers. The subsequent growth of the matinée performance began to attract women and increased attendance levels. From 1905 onwards the variety theatres of Preston presented, for the first time, twice-nightly performances, and at least two matinées a week, making the performances more attractive to women, textile and engineering workers on shift work and, increasingly, the middle classes.

This was a time when families had the opportunity to have a pleasant night out in Preston, put on their best clothes and meet their friends. Music-hall visits were social events attended by the family, friends and work colleagues. That twice-nightly performances became so common in Preston is perhaps testimony to the increasing patronage of a more sophisticated audience and propaganda by theatre owners that clearly aimed to attract the middle classes. At the opening night of the Royal Hippodrome, 'there were good houses for both twice-nightly performances.' The Empire capitalised on its advertising slogan, 'Get the habit – Twice Nightly', to attract regular patrons and the King's Palace had the performance times of 6.40 p.m. and 9 p.m as a permanent inscription on its terracotta exterior.

Voice from the Gods
'Are you interested in becoming a permanent booked seat patron for all twice-nightly performances at this theatre? Full details are available at the box office.'

Scene Two: Legendary Music-Hall Stars and Performance Styles

Though the economic foundations of music hall in Preston between 1905 and 1914 may have been less than secure in terms of the quality and range of entertainment, they were the town's golden years of variety, with many great music hall and theatrical performers appearing – including Florrie Forde, Vesta Tilley, Marie Lloyd, Houdini, Little Titch, Harry Champion and many more, including, of course, those aspiring stars employed on the 'bread and butter circuit'.

Harry Houdini first appeared in Vaudeville in his native America before coming to London in 1900 and the Preston Royal Hippodrome in 1906. He made his name synonymous with escapology and to promote his Preston performance demonstrated his skills by escaping from a locked cell in Preston Prison. His novelty act, when placed among a range of others (such as variety performers but also revue and integrated cinema interludes) shows how music hall had expanded as an entertainment form. The variety theatres were now licensed under the Theatres Act of 1843 for stage plays and the Preston Improvement Act of 1880 for music, singing and dancing. 'Variety' as a genre presented in the music halls of Preston took on elements that later ramified into revue and other entertainment styles. The culture of the circus continued to contribute to Edwardian music hall. Most of the Preston theatres produced acrobats, jugglers and strongmen as well as dogs and monkeys. On the 30 January 1905, only two weeks after it opened, the Royal Hippodrome was staging 'Woolford's Stage Circus', which suggests an attempt to draw upon an audience that had been accustomed to circus during the hiatus years.

The genre of performance integrated elements of Victorian music hall into the expanding Edwardian music hall.

Performance styles in Victorian and Edwardian Music Hall in Preston (compiled by the author)

Nineteenth-century King's Head Music Hall, Friargate, Preston	Twentieth-century Variety Theatres First performances
26 November 1870	16 January 1905, Royal Hippodrome
General manager: Mr George D'Arcy; band Mr Douglas, cornet, Mr McGowan, piano, Mr Collinson, flautist. The following talented artists will appear: Signor Sanguinetti with his marvellous and wonderfully trained performing birds, including Samson and Blondin, who will cross the rope each evening; Miss Ada Maitland, character vocalist and dancer; Mr and Mrs Gus Mangham; La Petite Bene, great Negro comedians; Barney O'Neil, Irish comic and dancer.	Charles Coburn (vocalist). Also appearing were Chard's Dogs; trick cyclists; acrobats; instrumentalists and singers.

22 May 1911, Empire Theatre

Marie Schulz (vocalist); Selvidge and Holland (comedy duo); Elsie Hulbert (clog dancer); Harry Rogerson (comedian); Harry Tate's company in *Gone Fishing* (revue); Bioscope presentation called *The Haunted House*. |
| 24 December 1870 | 12 August 1911, Empire Theatre |
| Concentration of talent for Christmas Miss Ada May, Queen of serio-comics; Harry Sinclair, baritone; Sam Redden, Negro comedian and stump orator; Sisters Vernon, operatic vocalists; Martin Brown, popular comic; Jessie Howard, serio-comic and dancer; La Petite Jennette, the infant wonder; George D'Arcy, comic and motto vocalist. | Less than three months after opening, the Empire was showing a week of films before reverting back to music hall.

6 February 1913, King's Palace (3,000 capacity audience) |
| 2 January, 1871 | *A Hot Time in Dogsville*. It featured performing dogs and monkeys enacting a New York street scene, supported by twelve Sunshine girls, (dance and chorus) ragtime and ballet numbers, comedy duo, acrobats, musicians and Harry Taft (whistling comedian). |
| Madlle Beatrice, Queen of the Globe, the only female performer in the world, will appear here. | |

The opening night at the King's Palace on the 6 February 1913 featured a circus-style act with Charles Barnold's 'dog and monkey actors' performing *A Hot Time in Dogsville*, which can be seen as an adaptation of a circus-style act for a more sophisticated audience. The eclectic 1913 programme illustrates how the latest entertainment styles, including dance in the form of ragtime and the twelve dancing girls, were touring Britain and being integrated into national music hall.

The increasing evidence of revue is a further sign of change. By 1911, sketches were already a part of the bill at the Empire's opening night with Harry Tate's company in *Gone Fishing*.

Sketches such as this developed into revue and revues were increasingly staged at most of the Preston music halls. In September 1914, the Empire presented Fred Karno's *The Hydro*. This was a typical revue with a London company featuring a real swimming bath and a bevy of beautiful girls with several musical scenic transitions. As a bright new approach, the family audience may have perceived this as variety although the beautiful girls swimming in the pool would no doubt have been especially popular with the male element! Nevertheless, contemporary critics were already beginning to perceive the sketches as a threat to the genre of variety. Archibald Haddon expressed what was missing in contemporary entertainment: 'In everything those veterans do or say or sing there is the human touch… Personality, which finds its expression most effectively in the solo turn, has been discouraged on the halls by the preference given to sketches, concert numbers and spectacular attractions and the result is that the halls are being dehumanised.' (*The Performer*, 7 August 1924)

Indeed, while revue was attracting a slightly more sophisticated audience, the emphasis on respectability had not gone so far as to eliminate the risqué element. Marie Lloyd, one of the most famous and controversial women of the era, had the innate ability to endear herself to all classes of society. She topped the variety bill at the Royal Hippodrome on the 30 October 1911. The *Lancashire Daily Post* gave a favourable report:

> Marie Lloyd heads a capital bill of fare at the Hippodrome this week and had a flattering reception at the matinée yesterday afternoon and in the two evening performances, large audiences appearing to hear the Queen of Comediennes. She did not disappoint her admirers. Bright, vivacious, tricky, and smart in song and action, she soon won favour, varying her songs for each performance and introducing new ones among old favourites. A catchy couple of numbers which tickled the fancy of the audience immensely yesterday, were 'Put on your slippers, you're here for the night', and, 'I haven't had a cuddle for a long time'.

Marie recaptured the music-hall atmosphere at Preston and in the absence of adverse reporting it sounds likely that her broad humour and double entendre was acceptable to all classes, including the respectable lower-middle classes.

The generic music-hall cast included comedians, a vocalist and dancer, an acrobatic comedian and a Houdini-style performer called Carla Mysto, 'the monarch of the manacles'. She was billed as the greatest success ever scored at the Hippodrome. Typically, she would have engendered a tremendous rapport with her Preston audiences with unashamed spontaneity and interaction with renditions of 'Oh Mr Porter,' 'My Old Man' and glancing towards the balcony to say hello to 'The Boy I Love up in the Balcony.' Marvellous stuff – Lloyd would have endeared herself to the working classes who would have felt a bond of empathy for her origins and the content of the risqué songs and sketches. As late as 1912, Lloyd was excluded from the Royal Command Performance because her humour was thought too broad, if not for royal house, at any rate for the new middle classes. Marie Lloyd died when only fifty-two, leaving behind a legendary reputation. Such was her popularity that in 1924, over twenty years after the music-hall's heyday, 100,000 people turned out for her funeral. To some extent, her 1911 Preston appearance might be seen as a legacy of the intimate atmosphere of the Victorian music hall.

Male impersonator Vesta Tilley became famous at all the leading halls up and down the country with middle-class families progressively participating as consumers. Upper-class figures were personified in songs such as 'Burlington Bertie', 'Champagne Charlie', and 'the Galloping Major' when Tilley brought her act to the stage of Preston's King's Palace on the 30 September 1913, direct from a successful season at the Palace Theatre, London.

As the range of popular entertainment broadened, music hall began to face stiff competition, most notably from the silver screen. This photograph shows the glamorous interior of the New Victoria Cinema's period café during the 1960s; it was managed at this time by Mrs Joan Hindle.

The end of the Edwardian era came when King Edward VII died on the 6 May 1910. Following the outbreak of war in early August 1914, the music-hall industry had to contend with the effects of the German offensive: darkened streets, the restriction on trains and the dearth of taxis, the curfew and finally the abundance of taxes both theatrical and general. This was to be the last stand of music-hall exuberance – and Florrie Forde boosted morale with the rallying song, 'Pack up Your Troubles in Your Old Kit Bag' when she appeared at the Royal Hippodrome, Preston, in October 1917. Preston had made its mark on the established circuit of music-hall icons such as Lloyd, Forde and the many others who appeared on the Preston stage between 1905-18.

The First World War increasingly saw variety theatres featuring ragtime, revue, opera, musicals, and drama to meet the changing tastes of audiences ranging from the working class to the bourgeoisie. These were substantial changes to the nature of generic music hall. As the range of popular entertainment broadened, music hall faced competition, most notably from cinema. Musicals and musical comedy began to prosper and, in drama, modern touring companies gradually displaced the nineteenth-century actor/manager.

Rivals to Generic Music Hall (compiled by the Author)

Name of Theatre	Performance type	Year
Theatre Royal	Civic use, drama, recitals, pantomime	1802–1866
	Music hall, drama, pantomime	1866–1869
	Musicals, Shakespeare, pantomime drama, melodrama, revue	1870–1911
	Cinema, drama,	1911–1920
	Permanent cinema	1920–1955
Gaiety Palace Theatre of Varieties	Music hall, circus, pantomime	1882–1888
Gaiety – change of name to Prince's Theatre and Opera House and latterly, the Prince's Theatre	Drama, revue, pantomime	1888– 1913
	Mainly cinema	1913– 1964
Royal Hippodrome	Music hall, circus, revue	1905–1957
	musicals, opera, drama, pantomime, variety	1918–1957
Empire Theatre	Music hall, opera, revue	1911–1919
	Drama, revue, opera	1919–1930
	Permanent cinema	1930–1976
King's Palace	Music hall, revue, drama	1913–1917
	Mainly cinema	1917–1939
	Music hall, revue, musicals, pantomime	1939–1955

Significantly, music hall had now to compete with the first silent films (including propaganda war films). In 1916 the feature length *Battle of the Somme* was not only the most successful propaganda film of the war, but also arguably the most successful British film of all time. The changing audience was postulated in *The Era* on the 6 February 1918. 'What will our audiences be like after the war. Who can tell? We shall welcome them, although they may not wear khaki. Our audiences will be made up of British men and women who have helped to free us from the world of the menace of the iron heel.' Primary sources indicate that the optimum period for music hall in Preston, when the town sustained up to three variety theatres, was between 1911 to the onset of the First World War, though it continued as an increasing anachronism until the mid-1950s.

Voice from the Gods

'Patrons please note your Palace (1938) programme: Our new, fully-licensed saloon refreshment bars at the rear of the circle and pit stalls are now open for the convenience of our patrons until 10 p.m.'

Curtain Up on Cinema

At the turn of the century the travelling fairgrounds and circuses visiting Preston showed the first films in tents and trailers. OHMY's circus integrated one of the first cinematograph performances in Preston during February 1901, when it used Gascoigne's Bioscope to project the Queen's funeral procession. In Preston, as elsewhere, the developing cinema industry was to have serious implications for the music-hall industry. At first cinema was thought of as a minor item within the musical-hall repertory and billed as the bioscope, but it was not long before this accommodation was seen as competition.

In 1907 a journalist wrote in the trade paper, *The Encore*: 'Seven years ago I pointed out to the profession that the greatest enemies the artistes had were the film merchants. The cinematograph picture shows have come to stay for each time an operator is employed two or three single turns are ousted.' By 1907 the Royal Hippodrome was utilising a bioscope to blend the silent pictures with music-hall acts. The bioscope was billed in Lloyd's 1911 Hippodrome performance featuring, 'some excellent views of holiday nights and incidents at Blackpool, shown on the bioscope.' As part of the music-hall package, the new Empire Theatre came complete with a projection equipment, and a bioscope presentation called *The Haunted House* was projected on the opening night at the Empire Theatre, and as early as August 1911, a week of films was shown.

The theatres were still dominant in 1911, with live music hall at the Empire and drama at both the new Prince's Theatre in the form of *Another Man's Wife* and at the Theatre Royal, where *The Builder of Bridges* was showing. Cinemas expanded after the First World War serving local communities in urban areas of the town as well as the town centre. However, in line with national trends, few bridges would be built between the emerging cinema industry and the music hall. The one exception to this was the Royal Hippodrome, which remained a live theatre throughout its existence.

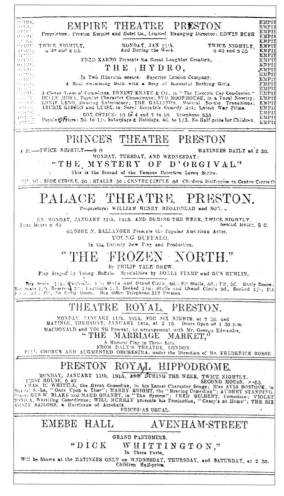

Left: The range of entertainment presented at Preston's theatres and music halls in January 1915. The Prince's and the Theatre Royal had cinema presentations while the tiny Emebe Hall boasted the grand pantomime, *Dick Whittington*. At the Empire there was a revue boasting a 'bevy of beautiful bathing girls'; meanwhile, the Hippodrome was staging variety and the King's Palace a dramatic production of *The Frozen North*.

The Preston-born cinema impresario, Will Onda, (real name Hugh Rain) played a key role in cinema provision in the town, opening Preston's first cinema in 1908 in Livesey's former Temperance Hall. This trend was in keeping with converting buildings such as theatres, churches and breweries into cinemas. An advertisement for the Temperance Hall for 22 June 1908 gave the following information: Matinée – Saturday at 1.45 p.m. and 3.30 p.m. Children 1d, 2d, 3d. Twice Nightly at 7 and 9; the family resort; the home of prize-animated pictures, Manager – Will Onda.

Will Onda was a former circus acrobat and entertainer who had travelled extensively abroad and had once appeared with Charlie Chaplin. A succession of managers followed Will's lead and cinemas expanded significantly in competition with music hall. In the same newspaper advertising Lloyd's live performance in 1911, three cinemas were advertising silent films: 'The Pictureland,' (Emebe Hall) the 'Marathon Electric Theatre' and the 'Imperial Picture Palace,' Church Street. The Emebe cinema adopted a theatrical role and was competing with the theatres in January 1915, with Christmas matinée performances of the 'grand pantomime *Dick Whittington*'.

Music hall accommodated film in its programming but also suffered direct competition from the emerging cinema buildings which undoubtedly resulted in a reduction of music hall and theatrical activity. As in most towns and cities, Preston's cinemas presented variety acts on stage, a form known as cine-variety. In 1920 Will Onda acquired a former brewery and named it the Picturedrome (later Palace Picturedrome). It had curtained boxes, a stage, circle, balcony and a roof resembling a Dutch barn. Local names for cinemas were not uncommon and the Picturedrome was also known as the 'Ranch House' because it specialised in showing westerns. Together the Prince's and Picturedrome Cinemas were billed as 'Will Onda's Pictures', featuring variety shows or soloists as well as the films. At the Prince's Theatre, 'Pictures and Turns' featured during the matinée performance in 1913, while the 'Picturedrome' presented Miss Rhoda Holding (contralto) after the main evening cinema performance in 1922. The impresario presented a further threat to the variety theatre, when in accordance with social change and to meet the growing demand for dancing he had the Regent Ballroom built next to the King's Palace in the 1920s.

Will perceived that the future was in films and the Prince's became a full-time cinema around 1915. Silent images of Charlie Chaplin were projected at the Prince's Theatre in 1917 in *Charlie Behind the Screen*, but on a Saturday afternoon Will presented his 'Mammoth Boxing Entertainment'. He put on the *Keystone Cops* with admission prices ranging from 1d to 3d and there were several shows a day. He was the first man in Preston to realise the value of serial films and the public queued to see, *The Exploits of Pearl White*, and *The Black Box*.

A diminishing music-hall genre at the King's Palace between 1913 and 1917 is apparent. After 1917 it sustained regular cinema use interspersed with occasional stage shows before reverting back to a full-time commercial live theatre in the 1930s. During 1917 it advertised: 'One continuous performance come what time you like stay as long as you like.' In the 1920s the theatre was advertised as 'The King's Palace of Music and Pictures'. Such was the popularity of cinema that on Christmas Day 1922, the Palace presented three performances of *The Three Musketeers* starring Douglas Fairbanks. Also during 1922 the Palace claimed the first and only screenplay made in natural colours – *The Glorious Adventure*, adding weight to the theory of over-expansion and illustrating how the music hall contributed to its own downfall. The huge King's Palace never really justified the investment made in it as a theatre, and with hindsight the objections and fears of rival theatre owners in 1913 that the industry was overburdened were vindicated.

Apart from cinema, music hall had to compete with the entertainment tax and a range of popular entertainment, especially sport and dancing. Oswald Stoll recognised the threat posed by radio in a report in the *London Evening News* dated May 1923: 'When broadcasting reaches a high state of perfection, the best singers, actors, lecturers and orators will be listened to by ten million people at a time. But all the lesser fry in artistry will be wiped out.' *The Gramophone Review* of

The Picturedrome Cinema was also known as the Ranch House, or Brackie, and was a familiar landmark situated next to Garstang Road. (Courtesy of Harris Reference Library, Preston)

1928, asked, 'Why, we ask ourselves, should we go out in cold and wet, into crowds, perhaps to see some entertainment that we cannot be sure of enjoying, when we have a comfortable chair and fifteen records of *Rigoletto* to entrance us'?

After the birth of cinema and a century before the multi-nationals of today, up to twenty-two cinemas were opened during the first half of the twentieth century to serve local communities in urban areas of the town as well as the town centre. There were some marvellous 'flea pits' in Preston: 'Fleckie Bennett' managed the Dominion Electric Cinema, a real 'laugh and scratch', and close by, his arch rival Alfred Wiles opened the Cosy Cinema in a converted chapel in St Peter's Street in 1921.

The Cosy was the place to be on a Saturday, as locals went to the 1d matinee, and in the evening a talent show was staged during the cinema interval, with homemade lemonade sold in jam jars. The official 'chucker out' was a certain Elijah Waddilove, who maintained order over the audience, many of whom would have worked in the mills, with a long pole! Admission to the Cosy for children was one penny or an empty jam jar. During the talent shows, locals who would attempt to sing, whistle in tune or dance in their new clogs, just like the music-hall performers – the prize, a jar of Elijah's lemonade and free admission!

Preston's town centre Palladium Cinema was the town's first purpose-built cinema to open its doors in 1915 with an incongruously titled film, *The Man Who Stayed at Home*. At the dawn of the talkie era in August 1929, the Palladium still boasted cine-variety, advertising 'sound silent attractions and good orchestral music always and on stage the Stan Wootton Trio and Albert Pryor, tenor vocalist.' Before Al Johnson's acclaimed *Singing Fool*, the advent of the talkies began in Preston at the Star Cinema. In 1929 the Star cinema boasted the slogan 'Preston's talkie cinema – the sound system supreme', for it pioneered short supporting talkie films.

Above left: The impressive Palladium cinema (1915-1968) was situated close to the Empire Theatre on Church Street. (Courtesy of the *Lancashire Evening Post*)

Above right: The Last Frontier, starring Victor Mature, appropriately heralded the former Empire Music Hall's demise as a cinema before conversion to a bingo hall. (Courtesy of the *Lancashire Evening Post*)

The Empress Cinema opened in 1929, coinciding with the first talkies. (Courtesy of the *Lancashire Evening Post*)

Preston goes 'talkie'

The transition to super cinemas began in 1927 upon the arrival of the first silent film with talkie dialogue and singing: *The Jazz Singer* starring Al Jolson. Surprisingly, the advent of the talkies began in Preston at the humble Star Cinema, Corporation Street, when it pioneered a short supporting talkie film and was dubbed during 1929 as 'Preston's talkie cinema – the sound system supreme'.

In anticipation of a cinema revolution, Provincial Cinematograph Theatres opened Preston's magnificent art-deco New Victoria, Fishergate, equipped with facilities for stage shows and cine-variety, on the 17 September 1928. Affectionately known as 'The New Vic' it had seating capacity for 2,120. The first feature film to be screened was the silent film called *Fazil*, starring Charles Farrell. At the opening night there was a half-hour stage show presented by the Regent Girls' acrobatic troupe, two male tap dancers, a contralto and Leslie Rogers on the Wurlitzer organ with the New Victoria Symphony Orchestra comprising twenty-two musicians. The popularity of the cinema organ had its heyday in the New Victoria, with its mighty Wurlitzer, on a rising platform and complete with resident organist. The New Vic also presented a pleasant surprise to patrons in having its own restaurant.

The impressive art-deco auditorium of the New Victoria Cinema was dominated by the awesome ceiling dome.

Significantly the first complete talkie, *The Singing Fool*, with Al Jolson was shown at the New Victoria on the 25 June, 1929. During the 1930s the phenomenon of the talkies brought a new batch of art-deco cinemas to Preston, which were given contemporary names like the Ritz, Plaza, Empress and Carlton. The uncompromising success of the talkies swept the town, threatening live entertainment as theatres such as the Empire finally gave way to film during 1930. A fruitful genre of British films began to appear featuring Lancashire comedians who had made an impact in the music halls of Preston, including the legendary Gracie Fields, George Formby as well as Preston's very own Janet Munro, who started off in repertory at the Royal Hippodrome before becoming a big movie star herself.

Artists continued the tradition of working the halls but they began to capitalise on their enormous popularity through the mediums of radio, gramophone and on cinema sound tracks. 'Our Gracie,' was an established music-hall artist by the time of her first 1931 film, *Sally in our Alley*, and gained increased popularity through films between 1936 and 1940. Gracie Fields had graced the Hippodrome stage in November 1922 with her husband Archie Pitt in a revue. George Formby (Junior) had appeared in revue at Preston Royal Hippodrome in 1924 and at the Preston Empire, during April 1929. Gracie and George were now exploiting the new film media with music-hall audiences overtaken by the expansion of the talkies. George Formby was one of the highest paid entertainers of the 1930s with a total of twenty-one films made between 1934 and 1946. His natural broad Lancashire accent and cheerful disposition symbolised the working classes. People could readily identify with his risqué songs and came to regard him as a gormless yet loveable Lancashire lad. Together with Gracie, playing a woman of humble origins working at the mill, they doubtless endeared themselves to town centre and community cinema audiences.

The traditions upheld at the local community cinema contrasted with the lavish cinemas such as the New Victoria. I remember that each of the Preston cinemas had their own characteristics and clientele, many of whom would attend on the same weekday, week after week, irrespective of the choice of film. The cinema with its neon façade and welcoming manager represented for thousands an escape from reality and going to the pictures was a cheap night out. One had to queue for what seemed like hours along corridors and into the street to see the main feature film, supporting film, adverts, news and trailer. As the audience came out of a film the manager would greet them and say, 'Av yer enjied it? See you next week!' Indeed at certain cinemas, patrons developed as personal a contact with the manager as with the local grocer.

At the 'Savoy' pandemonium was frequent during the pregnant pauses between reels or when the projector broke down. The manager (Ernie) sorted out unruly kids with their bags of parched peas or over-amorous members of the audience. Indeed, social precedents for the day demanded double seats for courting couples, and as I recall this cosy arrangement had a major part to play in blossoming romances, though usually interrupted by obsessive usherettes flashing their torches on the back rows.

Commensurate with 'Preston goes talkie,' the cinema industry reached its peak in the late 1930/40s. It was the age of Hollywood and the superstars and cinemas were hugely popular in wartime Britain with a huge demand for news. The cinema also played its part in presenting images of the monarchy to the population at large. At the Coronation of Queen Elizabeth II in 1953, television cameras were allowed inside Westminster Abbey for the first time. Approximately 20 million people watched the Coronation on television and 1,555,000 watched it at the cinema or in other public places, which were equipped with television screens. On Coronation Day the Empress Cinema, Preston, showed a continuous live performance of the Coronation. Like so many other cinemas and theatres, the Empress followed the national trend of closure during the 1960s with a phase as a Bingo Hall before it finally succumbed to television and changing tastes in youth culture.

Epilogue: The Later Years

Before the grey 1930s of economic hardship and another world war, music, operetta and touring plays all featured at the Preston Empire. This former music hall was undergoing a transitional phase as fashions cancelled each other out before it finally bowed out to cinema. Gertie Gitana, famous for her rendition of 'Nellie Dean', appeared in variety on the 9 November 1912, and likewise Lily Langtry trod the Empire's boards on the 4 September 1917. The twenties featured the musicals and operettas performed by the local amateur operatic societies so typical of the light musical stage of the decade. An interchange between the musical-hall stage and the theatre became the order of the day after the First World War as it changed frequently from musicals and drama to variety.

The Empire presented the latest plays from London and audiences of the 1920s witnessed the performances of famous actors and actor-managers. A season of plays starring the distinguished actor Frank Forbes-Robertson toured the provinces for six nights commencing on the 17 July 1922. It was billed as a personal visit by the distinguished actor in a new romantic play, prior to London production: *The Call of the Road* by George Norman and David Ellis, adapted from Tom Gallon's famous novel, *The Great Gay Road*.

The day of the 4 December 1922 saw a personal visit from Bransby Williams in a dual role as Mr Micawber and Peggotty with his full London company in *David Copperfield*. This particular actor-manager produced, acted and designed the special scenery and charged relatively high admission prices: lower boxes (to hold four) 30s, upper boxes (to hold four) 20s, grand circle 3s 6d, orchestra stalls 3s and 3s 6d on Saturday, stalls and promenade 2s, and 2s 4d on Saturdays, balcony 1s.

Sir Frank Benson and his company appeared in all three plays presented at the Empire theatre during the week commencing 29 October 1923. He appeared as Shylock – a Jew – in *The Merchant of Venice*; Caliban – a savage and deformed slave – in *The Tempest*; and Banquo in *Macbeth*. The value of Benson's services to the theatre can never be fully estimated and his passionate enthusiasm kept Shakespeare alive in the provinces even with the inclusion of that certain unmentionable play!

Fred Terry was another actor-manager who performed in Preston with his lovely wife Julia Neilson. At Preston he played the elusive Sir Percy Blakeney in the *Scarlet Pimpernel* during the week commencing 21 January 1924. 'They seek him here, they seek him there' – and alas, during the same year they sought economic viability for the impending fall of an Empire when two separate pleas for the ailing theatre were made by the managing director, Alan Young, through the *Preston Guardian* on the 22 March 1924:

Preston has a curious record in regard to its support of the drama and it is not a good one. Some time before the war the town had ceased to become one of the regular patrons of the theatre as distinct from the music hall and cinema, and though a valiant effort has been made to revive interest locally, an effort which has at time times shown splendid promise, there are unmistakable signs that the public response is by no means what it should be. As a fact there is a very real danger of Preston being struck off the visiting list of more than one famous theatrical producer, for the measure of support accorded some of the very finest productions recently has been so disappointing as to result in a heavy loss after a week's show here. The same thing happened in musical circles on the occasion of the recent visit of Sir Thomas Beecham and his famous orchestra and the only inference that can be drawn is that Preston is losing the taste for good music and plays…The indifferent patronage for recent productions is heartbreaking for any management. Surely there is room for entertainment of a higher type than the red-nosed comedian.

EMPIRE THEATRE, Preston

MONDAY, NOVEMBER 3rd :: Six Nights at 7.30

MATINEE on THURSDAY at 2.15

PERSONAL VISIT of

Arthur Bourchier

in an Entirely New Production of

HENRY BERNSTEIN'S

Famous Play

THE THIEF

(PRIOR TO STAGING IT ON HIS RETURN TO
THE STRAND THEATRE, LONDON)

with a

SPECIALLY SELECTED COMPANY

including MISS

Kyrle Bellew

JAMES CAREW

STELLA MERVYN-CAMPBELL

THE PRESTON AND DISTRICT AMATEUR
OPERATIC SOCIETY

(Affiliated to the National Amateur Operatic
and Dramatic Association)

PRESENT THE DELIGHTFUL MUSICAL COMEDY

A Runaway Girl

(By arrangement with The Gaiety Theatre Co., Ltd., London)

AT THE

EMPIRE THEATRE

PRESTON

MONDAY, 12th APRIL, 1926

AND FIVE FOLLOWING NIGHTS AT 7-30.

MATINEE THURSDAY AT
2-15.

Over £1,200 already given to Local
Charities.

BOX OFFICE at the Empire Theatre open daily from 10 a.m. to 9 p.m.

Typical programmes illustrating the diversity of operetta and dramatic productions at the Empire Theatre during the 'roaring twenties' (below).

Photo—Fredk. J. Ball, Friargate.   DANCERS.
Miss E. Murray, Miss M. Dawson, Mrs. L. Forrest, Miss K. I. Marks, Miss C. Jones, Miss A. I. Pye, Miss J. M. Walmsley, Mrs. E. H Abberley.

And on the 23 August of the same year:

> The decision as to whether the Empire theatre should be turned into a picture palace has ended as lovers of the legitimate theatre fervently hoped it would, but it remains to be seen whether the subject has been dropped permanently or merely for another year. It has been raised before this week's meeting of the theatre shareholders and obviously the decision must turn upon the measure of support accorded the Empire management in their wholehearted endeavor to stimulate the townspeople's for good plays and first class new productions in musical comedy and the like. No business can go on forever without making a profit, but there is every justification, for the optimism of the management that when trade conditions return to normal, locally there will be better times for the Empire. It is all a question of success or otherwise in gauging the public taste, but it is a tremendously difficult job for anyone to undertake, either in London or the provinces. Still the task has been narrowed down by the exclusion of variety shows from future entertainment at the Empire. Recent experience has shown that the day of the single turn is well nigh ended, at least as a really first class entertainment, and as the future booing of plays to be put on at the Empire indicate, it is clear that the management are anxious that Preston should have the very best productions that can be secured for the provinces.

Thereafter the theatre staged mainly dramatic productions as it was decreed to hold no more variety acts at the Empire – the writing was on the wall. During the summer of 1930, Frank Carriello's Repertory Company staged the last live performances with a season of plays, billed as 'your last chance to see your favourite stars before the Empire goes over to talkies'. The final stage performance was duly reported in the *Lancashire Daily Post* on the 4 August 1930:

> With the singing of Auld Lang Syne, the stage and audience linked over the footlights by the holding of hands, 'legitimate,' stagecraft took its farewell curtain at the Empire theatre on Saturday evening. Preston certainly bade farewell to the Empire as a theatre in worthy manner. Long before the first of the bi-nightly performances had concluded, there were long queues lined up at the pay boxes, and the foyers and stairways were thronged with those who had booked their seats. For the last show there was not an empty seat. Each box was occupied and through the rails of the gallery the occupants poked their faces, determined not to miss a single incident, however trifling, in what they regarded as the very last show.

The Empire was the third Preston theatre to transfer its permanent allegiance from the safety curtain of the theatre to the silver screen of cinema.

Voice from the Gods

'Patrons are asked to assist management by following the directions on tickets and occupying the seat indicated thereon with the least possible delay. A reminder to patrons that tea or coffee with biscuits can be reserved in the intervals, so please complete your programme slip now with your row and seat number and hand it to the usherette. Lion Ales are obtainable in the bar of this theatre.'

The Final Curtain for the Broadheads

During the 1920s William Henry resisted a quarter of a million pound offer from a film distributor wanting to purchase the whole chain of theatres as cinema outlets. His son Percy persuaded him that he was the only man in the country personally to own seventeen theatres and he should retain them. It was resolved that Broadhead's magnificent halls for the delectation of the people would be around a little longer, but sadly time was also running out for the creator of the Broadhead circuit.

Following the death of William Henry Broadhead in 1931, at the age of eighty-three, the Broadheads put up for auction their two Preston theatres on the 5 April 1933. The King's Palace was advertised as a 'talking picture theatre', with a bioscope chamber and re-winding room, dramatic and music, singing and dancing licence, ten dressing rooms, seating 2,340 in the stall, pit and balcony.

Following the event neither Preston theatre was sold, and both re-opened as variety theatres following the outbreak of war. The King's Palace remained as a Broadhead theatre managed by Percy Broadhead. However, the Royal Hippodrome was sold to Claude Talbot Entertainments, reopening in 1941 with a Jack Hilton revue called *Secrets of the BBC*. New owner Mr Claude Talbot proclaimed: 'It is the intention of the new management, to carry on the old tradition of the best in variety and musical comedy in the same atmosphere of comfort and cheeriness that made the old Hippodrome so popular.'

Both of the Preston theatres were affected by the trauma of six years of war. At the King's Palace the programmes advertised reduced prices for HM Forces and acknowledged the Nazi threats of bombing with the words:

ARP Notice: Should there be an Air-Raid warning, the Manager would announce the same from the stage so that patrons could leave the building if desired, or stay and see the show through, as the artists, orchestra and staff will carry on as usual after the warning has been given.

The atmosphere of wartime Preston is encapsulated when the Palace Theatre staged a variety show in aid of the Mayor's Fund for soldiers and a free buffet on Preston railway station, engendering confidence and optimism during traumatic times.

Variety acts predominated during and after the war, while lighting up the gloom of post-war Britain during 1947 were American musicals such as *Oklahoma*. A resurgence of interest in variety during the 1940s and '50s was evident with comedy reflecting the culture of northern humour and exploited by numerous northern comics. J.B. Priestly, in 1934, famously said: 'If you are a southerner, you may imagine that you have landed amongst a million music-hall comedians.' Many famous artists played Preston's theatres down the years including comics George Robey, Frank Randle, Ted Ray, Norman Evans, Jimmy James, Albert Modley, Sandy Powell, Hetty King, George Formby, and many more classic acts including singers Richard Tauber, Tessie O'Shea, Joseph Locke, Donald Peers, Harry Lauder, Paul Robeson, and a young Shirley Bassey, dubbed the 'sensational sepia songstress', who appeared at the Hippodrome in 1955; the prices began at 1s. Repertory was presented and widely acclaimed during the late 1940s and '50s. The Salberg Players first came to the Royal Hippodrome on the 14 July 1947. They were scheduled to last for only a few weeks, but after the initial run stayed for eight years, presenting around 365 plays. The company players included many stars, including such household names as Peggy Mount, Leonard Rossiter and John Barron.

The mid-twentieth century witnessed the permanent demise of the commercial variety theatre, attributed to changing social trends, the popularity of television and rising costs in all branches of the business. William Henry's grandchildren managed the substantially reduced Broadhead tour – Percy Baynham Broadhead Junior (also known as Sonny Broadhead) and Avril Broadhead. It lasted until the closure of the Preston King's Palace in 1955 and a few months later, the Salford Royal Hippodrome, trends that were by no means exclusive to provincial music hall.

The last performance at the King's Palace was a saucy revue called *Peaches and Screams* starring Ted Lune. At the final curtain, Sonny Broadhead announced the closure of the theatre before leaving it to Ted to entertain the audience until well after mindnight. Ted's catchphrase, 'Throw me the keys, I'll lock up', suddenly took on a particular poignancy for the audience and staff watching Ted's antics – the battle for the King's Palace was finally surrendered to new cultures and trends in popular entertainment.

THE
PALACE
THEATRE
Vicarage, Preston

Phone 3317

Palace Theatre kindly loaned by
Percy B. Broadhead & Son

SPECIAL
CHARITY
CONCERT

For the Mayoress of Preston's Effort for Sick and Wounded
Members of H.M. Forces.

at 3 p.m., Sunday, August 16th

Chairman: — — H. Garth, Esq., (Chief Constable)
Organising Secretary: — — Insp. J. W. Smith
Assistant Organising Secretary — — R. Pope, Esq.
Stage Management under the Direction of
Percy B. Broadhead Jnr. and Ernest Sims

PROGRAMME

1.—FANFARE .... Ketelby

2.—POPULAR OPERATIC MELODIES ....arr. Palmer

3.—JOAN FISHER with Band
Intermezzo from Cavalleria Rusticana

4.—NORMAN EVANS
The Popular Entertainer
(By kind permission of Jack Taylor Productions)

5.—BILLY SCOTT-COOMBER and JEANNETTE HAYLEY
with Billy Pearce at the Piano
(By kind permission of Jack Taylor Productions)

6.—TERRY WILSON
Radio's Light Comedy Star
(By kind permission of Feldman's Theatre, B'pool)

7.—DANCE ORCHESTRA OF THE LOYAL REGIMENT
with Joan Fisher and Judy Gray
(By kind permission of the Officer Commanding
The Loyal Regiment)

INTERVAL

8.—MARCH—"Bomber Command" ....Plater

9.—Music to Walt Disney's Film "Fantasia"...arr. Churchill

10.—WEE GEORGIE WOOD and DOLLY HARMER
Radio's Mother and Son
(By kind permission of Jack Taylor Productions)

11.—INSTRUMENTAL—Trombone ......Sergt. Denny
Piccolo ....Bdsmn. Greenwood
Xylophone ......L/Cpl. Barnfield

12.—TOM ROBINSON and ELLIE BALDWIN
"Songs from the Shows"

13.—DANCE ORCHESTRA OF THE LOYAL REGIMENT
with Joan Fisher and Judy Gray

14.—FINALE—"Flags of the Free".....................Sousa

GOD SAVE THE KING

The Mayoress of Preston and the Chief Constable express their very best thanks to the Artists and all who have given their
services in connection with this Charitable event.

Above, left and right: Programme of a Second World War charity show at the King's Palace in aid of sick and
wounded members of HM forces; doubtless Norman Evans and Wee Georgie Wood would have raised a laugh.

John Barron on stage at the Hippodrome whilst a member of the Salberg Players. (Courtesy of J. Barron)

'Sally' on the musical stage of Preston Hippodrome, presented by the Preston Operatic Society. (Courtesy of P.Vickers)

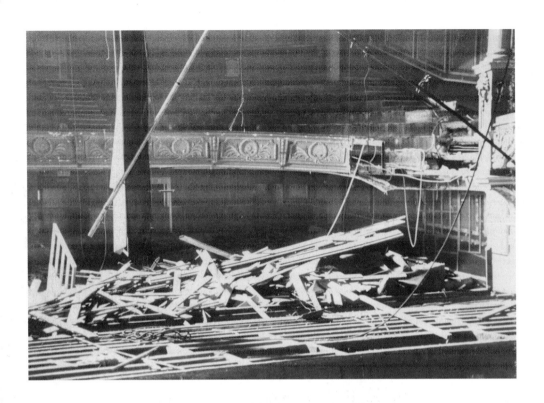

These pages: Final curtain as the Empire (opposite above), Hippodrome (opposite below), King's Palace (top of this page) and Prince's (above) Theatres are demolished. (Courtesy of the *Lancashire Evening Post*)

In May 1957, the owner of the Preston Hippodrome, Claude Talbot, went on stage to announce closure and addressed the biggest audience at the Hippodrome Theatre in years. 'The date 25th May 1957 should be remembered with shame by every citizen of this town who claims to enjoy the theatre. I don't think there will ever be a live theatre in Preston again.'

Preston's illustrious Royal Hippodrome never suffered the ignominy of conversion to a full-time cinema or bingo hall throughout its fifty-two year history. The old Hippodrome stood empty for two years and was demolished in 1959. Unlike the renowned Palais Garnier Opera Theatre of 1875, there are no stories of crashing chandeliers or subterranean lakes, though the Hippodrome was said to have had its own resident phantom; John Smith was a novelty juggler who died on stage in January of 1913, but came back to haunt the theatre and the C&A department store that was constructed on the same site.

Another link with music-hall's glorious past was depicted when Laurence Olivier played Archie Rice in the film *The Entertainer,* shot on location in Morecambe's glorious old Winter Garden's theatre and the ramshackle promenade of the Alhambra Theatre, appropiately cast as a seedy old music hall in terminal decline. Finally, the playwright John Osbourne used the decline of music hall as a metaphor to illustrate the decline of the power of the British Empire when reflecting on the national trend for music-hall closures in 1965: 'the music hall is dying and with it a significant part of England' – and who would disagree with that?

Accolade: The View from the Gallery

Voice from the Gods
'Ladies and Gentlemen: For your delectation and delight you are now invited to wallow in sheer nostalgia by perusing this splendid portfolio of contemporary music-hall programmes in a 'View from the Gallery.' Please witness the resurgence in post-war variety with veterans of the music-hall stage playing the provincial theatres in seaside resorts and in many towns and cities while retaining their popularity and emphasising the passing of an era. However, few would disagree that to this day Frank Matcham's masterpieces the Blackpool Grand Theatre and the London Coliseum are two jewels in the crown that epitomize the glories of the late Victorian theatre.'

THE PALACE THEATRE,

OLD VICARAGE, PRESTON.

Acting Manager—ERNEST SIMS.
Musical Director—EDWARD JONES.

Programme for Monday, May 17th, 1937, and during the week.   TWICE NIGHTLY at 6-40 & 8-45.   Saturdays & Holidays, at 6-30 & 8-40.

1. OVERTURE............" BHOYS OF TIPPERARY "

By Edward Jones and his Orchestra.

Welcome Visit

2. Miss Hetty King

The World-Famous Male Impersonator.

The Renowned Ventriloquist

3. David Poole

With JOHNNY GREEN presents
" THE SCHOOLMASTER."

A Novelty Sensation

4. The Famous Roadsters

B.B.C. and Recording Stars.

Singing, Dancing, Comedy, Harmony.

5. Felovis

THE CONTINENTAL JUGGLER.

In a Display of almost incredible Expertness.

6.   INTERVAL of Six Minutes.

The Orchestra will play

" RHAPSODY SLAVONIC."

7. Frank Wilson

The Australian Sundowner.

8. Marinoff's Canine Comedians

In their Famous Comedy Sketch
" VILLAGE SCANDALS."

The B.B.C's latest gift to Variety

9. Clifton & Young

The Swell Dame and the Tough Guy.

10. The Flying Flacoris

Sensational Trapeze Act.

WEEK COMMENCING MONDAY, AUG. 14th, 1944

HYMAN ZAHL presents

LANCASHIRE'S AMBASSADOR OF MIRTH

NORMAN EVANS

in a New, Jolly, Family Road Show

EVANS ABOVE

Supported by

Betty Jumel; Vic and Joe Crastonian; The Three Jacks;
Patino and Pesco; The Three Shades; Jass and Jessie;
Billy Pearce; Mabs Newnham's Twelve Sparklets, etc.

THE KING'S
PALACE THEATRE

VICARAGE & TITHEBARN STREET • PRESTON

THE USUAL POPULAR PALACE PRICES

FIRST HOUSE:
Doors Open 5-45, Commence 6-10.

SECOND HOUSE:
Doors Open 7-55, Commence 8-10.

The Prices include Entertainment Tax. Tel. Preston 3317

Matinees Commence at 2-15. Doors Open 1-45.

MEMBERS OF H.M. FORCES IN UNIFORM WILL
BE ADMITTED AT REDUCED PRICES.

Patrons Kindly Bring their Gas Masks

On SUNDAY Night at 7-15—Our Usual Sunday Concert
BOX-OFFICE NOW OPEN.

Telephone : BROUGHTON 5

BROUGHTON VILLAGE
BOARDING KENNELS

— FOR —

DOGS AND CATS

SEND YOUR ANIMALS TO THE COUNTRY FOR THEIR
HOLIDAYS.

ANY PERIOD (Every attention given to Sick and Parturition
Cases)

Proprietor — A. E. BLACKHURST

PROGRAMME   •   •   •   •   PRICE TWOPENCE

The Palace Theatre

VICARAGE, PRESTON

Proprietors ....PERCY B. BROADHEAD & SON
Manager: Percy B. Broadhead, Jnr.   Act. Manager: J. J. Newman
Treasurer: Arthur Chapman.   Musical Director: James White.

WEEK COMMENCING MONDAY, AUG. 7th, 1944

HARRY KENYON presents
A great holiday variety programme including
The Personal Appearance of the Famous Radio, Stage
and Film Comedian

ROBB WILTON

in his latest sketch
" THE DAY WAR BROKE OUT "
and Full Supporting Varieties.

A.R.P. NOTICE.—Should there be an Air Raid Warning the Manager will
announce same from the Stage so that Patrons may leave the building if they
desire, or stay and see the Show all through.   The Artists, Orchestra and Staff
will carry on as usual after the warning has been given.

When people say " How well
Glasses suit her" it's a fitting
by

JIM PROCTER
F.N.A.O.   F.B.O.A.   F.I.O.Q.

81 Ribbleton Lane, Preston
Consulting Optician

Phone: 3874.

Optician recognised by the Ophthal-
mic Benefit Approved Committee
for National Health Insurance
Optical Benefit.

FOR UTMOST COUPON
VALUES CALL AT

W. A. Sharples
THE LADIES' AND
CHILDREN'S OUTFITTER,

127, FYLDE ROAD.

A Large Selection to choose from
—at Prices to Suit All Pockets—
Your entire satisfaction is my
endeavour.

MOURNING ORDERS
A SPECIALITY.

TO PATRONS BOOKING SEATS. Booked Seats will only be
available for the Performance they are booked for.

A range of programmes from Preston. At the top, male impersonator Hetty King is at the King's, whilst in another programme from the same theatre during the Second World War, patrons are advised to bring their gas masks. Appropriately, Robb Wilton presented his famous sketch, *The Day War Broke Out*.

ROYAL HIPPODROME

TALBOT ENTERTAINMENTS LTD.
Licensee & Joint Managing Director...Claude Talbot
Booking Manager & Joint Managing Director :
Ivor E. Faull
Chairman.........................L. V. Hazlewood
Secretary..............................Harry Talbot
Stage Manager.......................James Pender
Musical Director.....................Walter Barry
General Manager....................Robert Winlow

WEEK COMMENCING
MONDAY, APRIL 29th, 1946

FRANK RANDLE
and Variety

PROGRAMME

During the war years, Prestons's Royal
Hippodrome offered an evening of variety
with Frank Randle (left), and above, in 1953,
the popular pantomime *Cinderella*; twenty years
later, household names such as George Formby,
Tommy Cooper and Charlie Chester were to
be found delighting holidaymakers in nearby
seaside resorts.

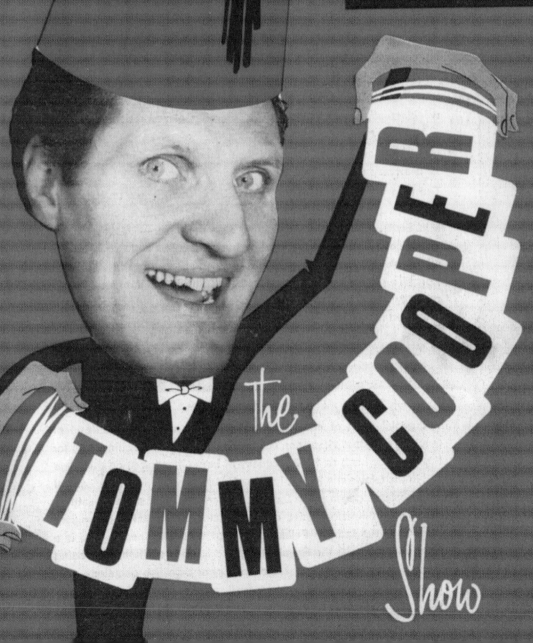

GEORGE & ALFRED BLACK
present

WINTER
GARDENS
PAVILION
BLACKPOOL

THE
TOMMY COOPER
Show

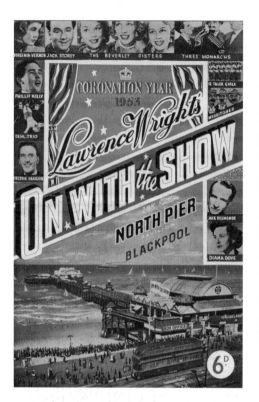

WEEK COMMENCING MONDAY, AUGUST 30th.

7-30 MONDAY to FRIDAY — Once Nightly 7-30

6-30 SATURDAY ONLY — Twice Nightly 8-30

PERSONAL
APPEARANCE
OF

FLORRIE FORDE

THE WORLD'S GREATEST CHORUS SINGER.

FRANK RANDLE
Famous Character Comedian.

WILBUR HALL
Comedy Feature of Jack Hylton's Band.

FOUR COMETS
Grace, Speed and Thrills on the Rollers.

JOHNSON CLARK
The Sportsman Ventriloquist.

TOLEDO, ELLY & JOAN
The Vivacious Trio.

SOUTH CHINA TROUPE
Wonder Equilibrists from the Orient.

AND STUPENDOUS VARIETY PROGRAMME

Morecambe Guardian Printing Dept.

Encore

Preston reflected national trends but had its own characteristics. The gin palaces, beer shops and early singing saloons were often one of the same set of premises staging primitive music-hall performances, and therefore the model of evolution of music hall in Preston equates with the notion of a progression: 'from a gin palace to a King's Palace.'

Preston was at the forefront of music-hall development and by 1839 its first concert hall was established. The movement against music hall was strengthened because of the local influence of Joseph Livesey and his followers, who advocated total abstinence and promoted counter-attractions. Nevertheless the 1860s and early '70s was a particular boom time for Preston's music hall with the opening of several new concert halls. Preston broadly follows the national pattern of growth but with a notable exception: there was no major variety theatre or properly constructed pub music hall in the town between 1889-1905.

Preston's three major variety theatres were built between 1905 and 1913 towards the end of the national music-hall boom, which lasted until the outbreak of the First World War. The opening of the Gaiety in 1882 marks a significant point within the mainstream framework of national music-hall development but diverges only six years later when it ceased to present music hall in October 1888. This marks a major step towards the demise of Victorian music hall in the town, an event atypical of similar sized towns during the late Victorian era. Preston failed to attract the big syndicate interest managed by theatrical entrepreneurs such as Moss Empires, McNaughten and Stoll during the 1890s. Paradoxically, Preston was devoid of a variety theatre to accommodate the golden years of legendary music-hall stars touring England's lavishly appointed new variety theatres, but eventually caught up in 1905 with the pre-eminent form of entertainment of the period.

Conversely, the evidence suggests there was an overprovision of theatre seats at the time of the battle for the King's Palace of 1913. With hindsight it can be seen that the objections of rival theatre owners were justified, that the economic equilibrium was disturbed and a saturation point in music-hall provision had already been reached. Research has shown that the coincidence of the over-ambition of the Broadhead syndicate with the rise of cinema signals the decline of music hall, especially as the King's Palace itself became a transitional full-time cinema by 1917.

The range of performance styles that gradually displaced music hall in Preston generally accords with national trends. The Empire is of particular interest as its performance styles ranged from music hall/revue, musicals, drama and finally cinema, thus illustrating the changing role of theatre in the twentieth century.

At the commencement of research into Preston music hall, I sought contemporary comment from Mr Alan Baker, the manager of the Preston Guild Hall and Charter Theatre, who informed me: 'Instinct tells me that so far as theatre is concerned, Preston has probably always been in the second division. Variety is dead nowadays and has been for a long time. Unlike the days of the old Hippodrome, traditional theatre entertainment seems to have little appeal in this city any more.'

To a certain extent, Mr Baker's words echo the comments of Whittle in 1821, who said, 'Drama never flourished to any great extent in Preston. To people of morose and narrow minds, who viewed theatrical performances as abuses that ought to be expelled from society as tending to feed the passions, and thereby nursing vice,'[29] and Alan Young, the managing director of the Empire Theatre in 1924, who attempted to analyse the lack of enthusiasm for theatre. An earnest playgoer said, 'Preston people require a lot of assurance that the show is a good one before they go to see it. They want half a crown's value for a shilling at the theatre.'

Whatever the truth of their observations for contemporary theatre, the period that begins with the first Preston free and easy until the closure of the last variety theatre is far from a 'second division' interest for the social historian. It is hoped that this book will be of value to those who share an interest in Preston's music hall and that, as a first study, it has contributed to the history of the town.

Voice From the Gods – *distinguished actor John Barron*

'The Old Preston Hippodrome was a fine place to work, with plenty of backstage activity, and a real theatre with a great atmosphere. We were a happy company and many of us had worked together before. The work we undertook may, on reflection, seem a bit rough and ready now by today's standards, cushioned as companies are by local and government subsidy. In the old days, it was the money taken at the box office one week that paid for the show the following week.'

And finally: 'Bring on the dancing girls' – a 1930s production of *Princess Charming* at Preston Hippodrome. (Courtesy of P. Vickers)

Bibliography

Primary Sources

Manuscripts held at the Lancashire Record Office:

Collection of Memorials and Petitions presented to the Magistrates, 1852, DPR 138/62
'Pitch and toss', in free and easy', 1838 Livesey, J. *Moral Reformer*, DDPR 138/48
Choral Music at White Horse Inn, Preston, 1840, DDP37/84
Preston Watch Committee Minutes, 1864, CBP 51/2
Plan of the new George Hotel, 1895, PR2/80
Detail of Preston Catch and Glee Club, 1819, DDPR 36/42
Plan of the Theatre Royal, 1898, PSPR2/224
Preston Pleasure Gardens, 1884, DDCM (6)
Details of sales by auction of Broadhead's theatres 1932/33, DDX 74/16/70
Annual Reports of the Rev. J. Clay, Preston Prison, 1824-1858, QGR/2-3 to 42
Census Enumerators' Reports
Moral Reformer, 1832-1833
Staunch Teetotaller, 1867, 1868

Parliamentary Papers at the Lancashire Record Office:

House of Commons Select Committee on Public Houses and Places of Public Entertainment, P.P. 1852-3
    XXXVII
Further report on the Licensing of Places of Public Entertainment, P.P. 1854, XIV
House of Commons Select Committee - Theatrical Licences and Regs. P.P.1866, XVI
1st Report, Select Committee, House of Lords, on Intemperance, P.P. 1877, XI
House of Commons Select Committee on Theatres and Places of Entertainment, P.P. 1892, XVIII

Newspapers and Periodicals:

The Era, 1838-1918
Lancashire Evening Post, 1886 –1957
Preston Chronicle, 1812-1893
Preston Guardian, 1844-1910
Preston Pilot, 1831-1877

Directories:

Barrett and Slater, Oakey and Mannex Directories of Preston, commence *c.* 1851
Whittle, Directory of Preston, commence 1841

Contemporary books at Preston Reference Library
Exhibits in the Harris Museum Collection, Preston

Oral interviews:

Major A. Burt Briggs (direct descendant of W.H. Broadhead), 22 January 1998.
John Barron, 4 March 1998.
Leonard Rossiter, 19 December 1977.
Jim Tattersall, 2 Februrary 1998.

Secondary Sources

Anderson, M. *Family Structure in Nineteenth Century Lancashire* (Cambridge, 1971)
Anglesey, N. *The People's Theatre* (Manchester, 1981)
Bailey, P. *Leisure and Class in Victorian England* (Toronto, 1978)
Bailey, P. *Music Hall: The Business of Pleasure* (Milton Keynes, 1986)
Bratton, J. *Music Hall Performance and Style* (Milton Keynes, 1986)
Cartmell, H. *Preston churches and Sunday Schools* (Preston, 1892)
Clemesha, H. *History of Preston in Amounderness* (Preston, 1912)
Cotterall, J. *Preston's Palaces of Pleasure* (Radcliffe, 1988)
Cunningham, H. *Leisure in the Industrial Revolution* (London, 1980)
Flintoff, T. *Preston and Parliament* (Preston, 1981)
Hardwick, C. *History of the Borough of Preston* (Preston, 1857)
Harrison, B. *Drink and the Victorians* (Keele, 1994)
Henderson, W. *The Lancashire Cotton Famine* (Manchester, 1969)
Hewitson, A. *History of Preston* (Preston, 1883)
Hindle, D. *Twice Nightly* (Preston, 1999)
Honri, P. *Working the Halls* (London, 1973)
Hunt, D. *History of Preston* (Preston, 1992)
Hunt, D. *Preston – Local History Guide* (Barnsley, 2005)
Joyce P. *Work Society and Politics* (Sussex, 1980)
Joyce, P. *Visions of the People* (Cambridge, 1991)
Kift, D. *The Victorian Music Hall* (Cambridge, 1996)
Mellor, G. *The Northern Music Hall* (Newcastle, 1970)
Morgan, N. *Vanished Dwellings* (Preston, 1990)
Poole, R. *Popular Leisure & Music Hall in 19th Century Bolton* (Lancaster, 1982)
Pye, H. *The History of Christ Church and Parish* (Preston, 1945)
Russell, D. *Popular Music in England 1840-1914* (Manchester, 1987)
Savage, M. *Dynamics of Working-Class Politics* (Cambridge, 1987)
Scott, H. *The Early Doors* (London, 1946)
Shiman, L. *The Crusade Against Drink in Victorian England* (Basingstoke, 1988)
Thompson F. *The Rise of Respectable Society* (London, 1988)
Vicinus, M. *The Industrial Muse* (London, 1974)
Walmsley, T. *Reminiscences of the Preston Cockpit* (Preston, 1892)
Walvin J. *Leisure and Society, 1830 –1850* (Harlow, 1978)
Walton and Walvin, *Leisure in Britain, 1780-1939* (Manchester, 1983)
Walton and Wilcox, *Low Life and Moral Improvement in Mid-Victorian England*; Walton, J. *Lancashire: A Social History, 1558-1939* (Manchester, 1987)
Whittle, P. *History of Preston* (Preston, 1837)

Articles in Books and Journals:

Bailey, P. 'Naughty But Nice,' in Booth, M. and Kaplan, *The Edwardian Theatre* (Cambridge, 1996)
Crump J. 'Provincial Music Hall,' in Bailey, P. *Music Hall* (Milton Keynes, 1986)

Cunningham, H. 'Leisure,' ed. Benson J. *The Working Class in England*, (1985)

Earl, J. 'Building the Halls,' in Bailey, *Music Hall* (Milton Keynes, 1986)

Reid, D. 'Popular Theatre in Victorian Birmingham,' ed. Bradby, D. *Performance and Politics in Popular Drama* (Cambridge, 1980)

Russell, D. 'Varieties of Life: the making of the Edwardian Music Hall' in Booth, M. and Kaplan, J. *The Edwardian Theatre*, (Cambridge 1996)

Smith M. 'Lancashire Cotton Towns,' ed. Bell, *Victorian Lancashire* (London, 1976)

Stedman Jones, G. 'Working-Class Culture in London 1870-1900' *Journal Social History* 7, 1974

Waters, C. 'Manchester Morality and the London Capital,' in Bailey P. *Music Hall* (Milton Keynes, 1986)

Waugh, E. *Home Life of the Lancashire Folk, 1867*

Endnotes

1 Russell, D. *Popular Music in England* (Manchester University Press, 1987) pp. 72–80
2 Kift, D. *The Victorian Music Hall* (Cambridge University Press, 1996) p.3
3 Vicinus, M. *The Industrial Muse* (London, 1974) p. 239
4 Stedman Jones, G. 'Working-Class Culture in London 1870-1900' in *Journal Social History* 7, 1977 pp. 460–508
5 Russell, D. *Popular Music in England* (Manchester University Press, 1987) p. 80
6 Bailey, P. *Leisure and Class in Victorian England* (Routledge and Kegan Paul, 1978)
7 Bratton, *Music Hall Performance and Style* (Open University Press, 1986)
8 Bailey, P. *Music Hall: The Business of Pleasure* (Open University Press, 1986) pp. xiii –xv and p. 1
9 Poole, R. *Leisure and Music Hall in Nineteenth Century Bolton* (Lancaster, 1982)
10 Reid, D. 'Popular Theatre in Victorian Birmingham,' in *Performance and Politics in Popular Drama* ed. Bradby, D. (Cambridge University Press, 1980) pp. 65-85
11 Crump, J. 'Provincial Music Hall in Leicester,' in Bailey, P. *Music Hall: The Business of Pleasure,* (Open University Press, 1986) p. 53
12 Waters, C. 'The Battle over the Palace of Varieties' in Bailey, P. *Music Hall: The Business of Pleasure,* (Open University Press, 1986) p. 141
13 Russell, D. 'Varieties of Life: the Making of the Edwardian Music Hall' in M. Booth and J. Kaplan, *The Edwardian Theatre* (Cambridge University Press, 1996) p. 61
14 Mellor, G. *The Northern Music Hall* (Frank Graham, 1970)
15 Anderson, M. *Family Structure in Nineteenth Century Lancashire* (Cambridge University Press, 1971) pp. 23-72
16 Sir Gilbert Scott's magnificent Gothic town hall was not completed until 1867 and superseded the old 1781 town hall referred to by Dickens in around 1853.
17 Walton, J. *Lancashire: A Social History* (Manchester University Press, 1987) p. 244, 284
18 See also Honigmann, *Shakespeare: The Lost Years* and the research undertaken by Professor R. Wilson of Lancaster University.
19 Whittle, *History of Preston* (Preston, 1821), pp. 95-96.
20 'Habits and Customs of the Working Classes', *Fortnightly Review*, 11 July 1867.
21 *Preston Chronicle*, 17 March 1866, 16 March 1867 and 5 September 1868.
22 *Preston Chronicle*, 11 February 1865.
23 Clay J. *Annual Report House of Correction*, LROQGR2/3/4 1850.
24 Joyce P. *Work, Society and Politics* (Methuen Press, 1982) p. 171, 286.
25 *Staunch Teetotaller* No. 7, July 1867, pp. 49-50.
26 Walton, J. *Lancashire: A Social History* (Manchester University Press, 1987) p. 299
27 Bailey P. *Music Hall: The Business of Pleasure* (Open University Press, 1987) p. xiii
28 Russell D. 'Edwardian Music Hall', in Booth and Kaplan, *The Edwardian Theatre*, (Cambridge University Press, 1996) p. 65.
29 Whittle, P. *History of Preston* (Preston) p.93.
30 Bratton, *Music Hall Performance and Style* (Open University Press, 1986).
31 *Memorial Primitive Methodist School, Preston, 1852*, LROMSSDPR 138/62

Index